Blair C. Adams
*Selected Writings
and Quotations*

Blair C. Adams
Selected Writings and Quotations

Colloquium Press
Elm Mott, Texas

Copyright 2023
Colloquium Press Trust

All rights reserved. No part of this publication may be reproduced, stored in a retrieval system, or transmitted in any form by any means, electronic, mechanical, photocopy, recording or otherwise, without the prior permission of the publisher, except as provided by USA copyright law.
062423

ISBN: 978-0-916387-33-4

Printed in the United States of America

Contents

Foreword. xiii

Preface xvii

Part I
What Kind of Culture?
Exodus Beginnings. 2
Discovering True Riches 4
Resonance of Love 6
The Fruit of Living in Harmony 7
Transparency of Simplicity 8
Single-Mindedness toward God 10
Great and Wondrous Gifts. 12
Work That Is Sacred 14
Choosing the Right Dreams 16
A Particular Culture 17
Garden of God 18
"A Garden Enclosed" 20

Part II
Covenant Love
An Unfolding Love. 22
Chesed: The Daily Walk of Prose 23
Necessity of Covenant 25
Self-Conquering Love 26
Life's Inevitable Tests 28
The Harmony of Human Relationship. 30
Life Inheres within the Form 32
We Love That Which We Trust 34
"Until Death Do Us Part" 35
An Enduring Sense of Awe. 36
Transcendent Faith for the Journey 38

Stepping into the Unknown 40
Complementarity 42
Union between God and His People 44
Possessed by Love 46
Agony unto Ecstasy 48
The Greatest Witness 49
Love Is as Strong as Death 51
Love Binds Together 52
The Power and Peril of Love 54
Protection Provided through Covenant 55
Vulnerability within the Protection of Covenant . . . 56
The Humility of Love 58
The River of Love 60

Part III
Christian Character
The Meaning of "Character" 62
Knowledge or Love? 63
Honor versus Dishonor 64
Honesty 65
Discipline 66
The Fear of the Lord 67
Hearing and Obeying 69
Dangers of Pride 70
Self: Survival or Sacrifice? 72
The True Nature of Humility 73
Humility Blossoms into Peace 75
Pride's Emptiness 76
Asleep to the Transcendent 77
Character Dismantled Board by Board 78
The Call to Perfection 80

Part IV
"Teach Them to Your Children"
Aiming the Arrow 82

Educating the Whole Person. 83
Parental Relationship 84
Parental Initiative 86
The Strength of Conviction 88
Opposite Views, Opposite Gods 89
Education: The Conflict for Control. 90
Which Kingdom and Culture?. 92
Which Kind of Knowledge? 93
Teaching Children to Seek God 94
Going to the Source 96
Overcoming That We Might Give 97
Inheritance of the Anointed Word. 98
The Maturity of Wisdom. 99
Wisdom Builds Her House. 101

Part V
Work as Worship
What Is Craft? 104
Manual Is Not Menial 105
Labor Is Worship. 107
The Sacredness of Work 108
A Response to the Highest Calling. 109
Recapturing the Meaning of Work. 111
Art Expresses Religion 112
"Why Do You Do It?" 113
Beauty: The Outshining of Order 114
Work That Speaks 115
Art as Virtue 116
The Craftsman as a Conduit 117
To Express the Love of God 118
Responsibility Makes a Craftsman. 119
Serving Creation 120
A Calling. 121
"For the Joy Set before Us" 122

Part VI
The "Full Declaration"

Knowing the Only True God	124
The Central Revelation of the New Testament	126
Complete Unity	127
The Full Declaration	129
The Unfolding Revelation of God's Nature	130
God's Authority	132
Jesus' Twofold Nature	134
Spirit and Flesh	135
The Power of Redemption	137
God's Mercy Unveiled	138

Part VII
"My Sheep Hear My Voice"

The Resonance of Truth	140
Meaning Comes through Relationship	142
Two Contrasting Ways of Knowing	144
"That You May Know Him . . ."	145
The Scripture Cannot Be Broken	146
A New Language	147
"Spirit and Truth"	148
A Prereflective Sense of Truth	150
Hearing the Whole	151
Recognizing the Truth	152
Proper Relationship to the Whole	153
A Tangible Experience of God's Love	154
The Ultimate Criterion forKnowing Truth	156
The Voice of the Spirit	157
Facts without Meaning	158
The Illusion of Impartiality	159
Changing What Is Possible	160
The Essence of Conviction	162
Constraint Brings Compression	164
One Crucial Truly Free Choice	165

God Hears Your Prayers 166

Part VIII
"As the First Gleam of Dawn"
Facing Life's Unknowns 168
Starting a Spiritual Revolution. 169
"From Faith to Faith" 171
Beyond Our Imagination. 173
Flawed Perceptions .174
Following Christ. 175
Hearts "Set on Pilgrimage". 176

Part IX
Strength through Weakness
The Path of Vulnerability 180
Necessity Creates Possibility. 181
Fashioning Human Life into Art. 183
The Pounding of the Clay 184
"In the House of Mourning" 185
The Meaning of Suffering 186
Yielding to a Greater Design 187
Hidden in the Secret Place 188
A Form to Hold the Content of Love 189
A Race between Two Reductions 190
Surviving into Old Age. 192
Beating Death at Its Own Game 193
The Transforming Power of Love 195
Love That Cannot Be Canceled 196
Testimonies of Triumph. 197
Far Greater Freedom. 199
God's Purpose for the Church 200

Part X
Repentance unto Life
Grafted into the Root 202

Becoming Centered in Christ 203
Seeking Transparency 204
Repentance Brings Acknowledgment 205
Acknowledging Harder Truths. 206
Ceasing from Excuses 208
Cutting Off Sin. 210
Dying to Double-Mindedness 211
Breaking Self-Will 213
A Made-Up Mind. 214
Digging to Bedrock. 215
An Ongoing Need for Humility 217
Dying Daily 218
Dying to Death 220
The Acceptable Sacrifice 221
Dead Works Bear Plastic Fruit 222
Discipling Relationships 223
Resurrection Power 225

Part XI
"I Will Not Leave You Orphans"

Explanation over Experience? 228
Experiencing the Numinous 229
An Unveiling 231
Beyond Mere Religion 233
In the Cool of the Day 235
"Yes, God, Yes". 237
Spirit and Truth 238
Theology or Relationship? 240
A Demonstration of Power. 242
The Importance of Frames. 243
New Frame, New Language 245
The Firstborn of Many Brethren 246
Empowerment as Sons 247
Revealed unto Babes 248
A Promise for Believers 249

The Promise Poured Out. 250
Living by the Power of God 251

Part XII
Fitly Framed Together
Laying Down Our Works 254
Clearing the Obscuring Rubble 255
Laboring to Enter God's Rest 256
Grace Working in Us 257
Leaving the Realm of Abstractions. 258
Tangible Love-Service 259
Becoming Transparent Vessels. 260
"Each Part Does Its Share". 261
Growing to a Place of Maturity 262
Meaning Found in Relationship 263
Suddenly Reoriented. 264
"Complete in Him" 265
Commissioned to Go Forth 267
God's Manifold Wisdom. 268
"Wisdom Builds Her House". 269
Building a Dwelling Place for God. 270
Perfectly Coordinated 272

Part XIII
"Radical Possibilities"
"Progress" or Simplicity? 274
Bedrock Alone 275
Aporia: Catalyst for Radical Change 277
Flying or Falling? .279
Radical Possibilities 280
Preparing to Offer Hope 281

Part XIV
"A City Set on a Hill"
Called Out 284

Authentic Unity 285
A "Spiritual Convenience Store"? 286
A Means for Healing 287
Self-Sufficient in Christ 288
A Functioning Alternative 289
The Mountain of Inheritance 290
"In Your Midst" 291
Making the Most of Every Opportunity 292
Ever-Clearer Contrast 293
Culture of the Covenant 294
Faithful to the Form 295
New Covenant Covering 297
The Experience of Covenant Love 299
Living in Harmony 301
Progressing in Unity 302
A Call to Repentance 304
A Call to Restoration 305
Vessels of Honor 307
The Aquifer of Love 309
Dying to Distraction 311
Words to Stand By 312

About the Author 315

Bibliography 323

Endnotes 331

Foreword

In my earliest memories, I hear the rhythmic creaking of Dad's gold tweed recliner. Dad kept the rocker in motion with his heel, a sheaf of papers tucked up under his bearded chin. Extending a manila folder in his left hand, he scrawled across its face. Sometimes he gazed off into space, collecting the words like swirling, sunlit dust particles out of the air.

I loved the sound of his scratching pen. It was the sound of home, of Dad and things familiar. Wanting to be just like him, I'd perch on a little stool beside his chair, stick my heel out on the floor in front of me and hold up a yellow legal pad I'd found somewhere. I always looked for a red pen like his to scratch across the paper. Focused on keeping that rhythmic sound, I filled page after page with loops, squiggles and scrawls. I didn't know how to write yet, but I thought it was "literature" (the term we often used to refer to the entire scope of Dad's work), and I was playing my part. (My younger brother, on the other hand, was known to say in his early years, "When I grow up, I want a *real* job! I want to *work*—not just sit with papers in my lap all day.")

Sometimes Dad would leave his ancient rocker and pace the room, manila folder in hand, jotting down thoughts as he walked. Other times, when we hiked in the woods, he'd pull a small pad out of his shirt pocket and jot down impressions. He even wrote in bed. It was a passion and a calling for him; he couldn't stop writing.

In our family of ten kids, life was full with schoolwork, gardening, canning, cooking, animal chores and crafts. Mealtimes at home always held special importance. My dad viewed all of life as a classroom and an opportunity to learn. So meals often became full-fledged lessons—not usually because he planned a class, but because he never missed an open door or an opportunity. And those impromptu lessons were the best! If we were devouring a steaming mountain of Colorado potatoes dripping with home-churned butter, we might learn about the Irish potato famine. If someone came in from turning garden beds, we'd learn about the benefits of French biointensive horticulture. Discussions on modern or ancient history, evolution versus creation, and whether or not politics fell within a Christian's sphere of duties all had their place. If anyone knocked on our door to drop something off during dinnertime, Dad almost always squeezed in an extra chair, and they ended up with a heaping plate of food and likely an opportunity to join in a geography, history or Bible lesson.

All ten of us were home-schooled, and writing workshops with Dad were my favorite part of our schooling. He'd usually start by reading us examples of good writing, which meant lots of stories. Then we all wrote together, including Dad, and afterward read our writings out loud to each other. Those writings provided some of my first glimpses into my brothers' hearts as well as my own. Dad describes my brother in one of those workshops with better words than I could:

> "His face is still pale from winter but is soft as a cloud now in his musing excitement. Recently, he did a writing assignment that began, 'When I grow up, I want to be . . . .' He had to finish the sentence and then read it out loud. I was in the room sitting in my rocking chair reading my own book when he read it to his mom, who teaches him at home. He started reading forcefully with a beaming smile, 'When I grow up I want to be a good man,' and then very softly, with serious face and tight voice, '. . . like my dad.' I immediately positioned the book

of Wendell Berry poems more in front of my face and choked down my feelings. He lifted his paper in front of his face and did the same. Nothing else was said.

"When he catches me staring at him now, his face lights up in a brilliant, gentle smile of perfectly even teeth with a gap here and there from missing baby ones."

Dad believed that writing with "real voice" could reveal our inner selves or possibly illuminate truths about God, His creation and each other. Thus he wasn't afraid to call us out when our writing seemed affected or plagiarized in some way. But he also lavished praise for authenticity and encouraged us when our words resonated with the truth.

Some of the writing exercises in the *Right Words* curriculum book came from our family's real-life attempts to learn its lessons. Most of Dad's writing expressed or addressed actual needs or real concerns. *Building Christian Character*—his bestselling title—was born of Dad's desire to help Mom fulfill her responsibilities and guide their ten children to become mature, Christian adults. Many of his theological books originally grew from conversations with guests, letters to relatives, concerns within the church and Sunday preachings as Dad wrestled to rediscover the answers from the Word of God to equip believers seeking to live authentic Christian lives.

Dad read to us often—everything from the Bible to Wendell Berry poems, from Tolstoy to Pat McManus hunting comedies, and from many of his own writings. He always asked if we understood it. Could we explain it back to him? How about we look up that word in the dictionary? Then he would revise and simplify his work until we could grasp the meaning.

I confess I had a love-hate relationship with editing. On the one hand, I hate to admit how many times in those early years I shed tears when I received a writing back from Dad bleeding with red ink, the margins full of questions and suggestions. Dad would ask, "Why does that upset you? My revisions of my own writing are redder than that! If there was nothing of value in your writing, I wouldn't have bothered to make a mark on it. But when there's a nugget of truth, it must be unearthed, sanded and polished until it's the gleaming jewel it was meant to be."

On the other hand, there were many times that we loved editing. Sometimes Dad typed our writings into the computer and highlighted a sentence. "Now, how can we say that better?" he'd ask. My brothers and I would compete to volunteer the zestiest verb, the most concrete noun, the most vivid adjective. It became a game to "cinch in the belt" of our writings and make them concise and cogent.

As we envisioned compiling this book of selected quotations from Dad's writings, we hoped these pages might provide another place where a few of the jewels of truth that Dad spent his life expressing could be shared—in his loving memory and for the glory of the Author of his faith.

I only regret that he couldn't be here to help me edit this foreword!

—Amanda Lancaster

Preface

This book is a collection of excerpts drawn from the writings of Blair Adams. Although thematically diverse, this compilation is neither an exhaustive anthology of Blair's writings nor an extensive portrayal of the beliefs of the church he founded, Heritage Ministries. It is composed, instead, of submissions from scores of Blair's readers who shared their favorite passages from the vast body of his published works, spanning nearly five decades. So the intention is to pass on to you, the reader, these easily digestible, thought-stirring selections in one compact volume.

The excerpts are grouped into fourteen themes, with each theme encompassing an assortment of subtopics. Some selections, such as transcriptions of messages Blair preached, have been slightly adapted from their original source to accommodate their use in this format. To facilitate delving deeper, relevant Scripture references can be found in the footers of the pages, and a detailed bibliography provides further information on each source title. All titles are published by Colloquium Press.

Part I
What Kind of Culture?

Exodus Beginnings

Urban restlessness and disillusionment can at times incite a greater attentiveness to the "old" land's soundless calling, and the end result may even be an exodus from one kind of country, one kind of America, to another. So it was with us who, at the time, lived in America's broadest and then most dangerous urban sprawl (the New York megalopolis). We first asked ourselves, "Am I hearing things?" We raised our heads from our busy labors in our cubicles of glass, concrete and chrome in the "new" America to see if we had really heard anything speaking to us from the old.

The sound seemed to ring forth faintly again and again. We wiped our brows and turned our heads for a moment from our assembly lines, our loading docks, our grocery stand produce. We loosened our neckties, or stepped out of one high heel to stretch our toes. We laid down our calculators and pencils. We stepped away from our keyboards. We rose and gazed more closely through the glass eye of our city cubicles. We stared down at the teeming asphalt, then across to the soot-stained buildings and looming monoliths which held other brick or concrete caverns like our own.

We squinted up past the maze of utility lines and the labyrinth of building tops stretching as far as the eye could see. And, through the haze of smog, white clouds seemed to be scudding across what appeared to be light blue skies with specks of something that seemed alive and scattered against the clouds—*pigeons*! Of course we'd in some sense noticed the skies, the clouds and the pigeons before—but only vaguely, almost unconsciously, as if asleep. And so somehow it was different this day, like the first day of creation. A strange, vibrating curiosity had taken hold of us. What was this mysterious longing stirring so within us? Whatever it was, we could not resist its call. So eventually we stepped forth from our urban "America," as if in a dream, and began to tentatively follow the silent sound.

—*Why We Live in Community*

Discovering True Riches

Here, we sing no "song of self" but one of roots and soil and horses and blue sky, of the scents and sights of earth and creatures—and of all of it coming together in the great community of life, the communion of the great God. Here, we always sing a song of the "Other," of all that lies beyond the self, of all that collaborates in life and in the conspiracy of caring. And so we become part of that call, reaching toward all of life, inviting it to come out of every dark hole, to dance and sing in the sunlit fields of God.

—*A Time of Harvest*

A land-centered way of life provides much more than a means to enter into relationship with natural creation. It is the context of close personal relationships. As we work together with our brothers and sisters—farming and gardening, preserving foods, working at crafts—we grow close to one another. As much as we love the land and cherish the intimacy we have found with it, we appreciate even more the way this land-centered life has enabled us to learn to share our lives with one another. We've discovered that it's not so much what we do to the land but what the land does to us and to our relationships with God and one another. This sharing of life defines the Greek New Testament word *koinonia*, a sharing that finds its basis in our service to one another in love.

Rather than basing our relationships on "what you can do for me," we seek to base them on what we can do for each other. Our relationships of service bring us so close as to weave our hearts together: "Above all," Paul said, "love each other deeply . . . . Each one should use whatever gift he has received to *serve others*." Because our lives in community so intertwine, even the most apparently mundane situations, tasks and relationships of everyday life offer us opportunities for growth into the "true riches" by providing the form through which God's love can flow.

—Koinonia Country

Resonance of Love

We find that as we offer our lives—our time, our hearts, our resources—yielding to the felt capacity to see and meet the needs in others, a rich daily experience of fellowship draws us into the life of the community. Much of this fellowship takes place in the context of our work, chores and everyday activities, but we also enjoy special times together—moments aside, picnics, evenings of singing and laughter, as well as larger, greater occasions.

After chores and the responsibilities of the day and season, and as we find the opportunity, folks will get together in the evening at someone's home or in the community building on the common land. Then the sounds of human voices, of fiddles, banjos, guitars and tambourines, ring out in the night as we sing songs, break bread, talk and laugh. Time and again, whether our conversation remains light or takes a serious turn, some common chord will strike in all our hearts, vibrate and resonate between us and fill the room with its presence, until it becomes His presence. This feeling is the most distinctive part of our life, and yet it is so difficult to explain or put into words. It is, of course, love; but it is a love so tangible and numinous that it can at times be physically felt, a vibrating resonance that comes from above and beyond us. Even the least "superstitious," those furthest from any belief in God, have admitted to feeling this resonance among us at times. We, of course, call it the love of God, and we see its clearest expression in the face of Jesus. That's how tangible and personal it has become for us.

—*Koinonia Country*

The Fruit of Living in Harmony

> *It's true: living is sometimes hard—when you grow your own food, give birth in your own home, educate your own children, take care of your own aging parents or grandparents. But, you see, the rewards are so great. For the fruit of living is more life.*
>
> —A Journey Home

Creation is God expressing qualities of His own nature through His Word. Through this Word, He has formed and ordered all things so that each will resonate as an instrument in sympathetic vibration—each will sing its part in the song—within the musical range that God has ordained for that part of creation as it interrelates within the context of the whole. And when every element of creation resonates in harmony with its "musical" range, the total result of all creation "playing" together will be the eternal symphony that declares fully God's glory, the cosmic Song. Everything that sings this song has been made beautiful by God *in its own time*.

—*Wisdom's Children, Book Two*

Eccles. 3:11

Transparency of Simplicity

But I fear, lest somehow, as the serpent deceived Eve by his craftiness, so your minds may be corrupted from the simplicity that is in Christ.

—2 Corinthians 11:3

To live the simple life does not mean living a destitute life deprived of essential needs. Simplicity is to us good in a specific sense, just as purity, honesty, kindness, loyalty, generosity, courage and love are good. Simplicity's good resides in the fact that it is the "virtue which regulates our attitude to material things." It is rooted in and sustained by love, which is to say it is rooted in and sustained by God. So simplicity is to us holy. It is the same attitude toward the material world of which Jesus spoke when He said, "Blessed are the poor in spirit, for theirs is the kingdom of heaven." When our attitude toward material things is governed by simplicity, we may seem to lose a few things of that world, which usually only clutter our lives and choke out love, but what we gain is a kingdom of love, peace and joy—a realm of relationships with God, nature and our fellow man, a kingdom never known to us before.

Like all the other virtues named above, only love can bring us to simplicity, but the teaching of simplicity—to give rather than to receive, to lose one life that we might find a better, to possess less while having more to enjoy—this is to us a positive teaching, not a negative one (although at times it distresses us to see how far short we fall of our own goals and standards). Essentially, then, the form of this teaching is to us no more a "do not" code than a

---

1 John 4:8, 16; Rom. 14:17; 1 Tim. 6:6-11; Heb. 13:5; Phil. 4:11-13; 2:1-8; Acts 4:32-33; 20:35; Luke 9:23-24

sculptor's chips and the marble dust on the floor represent the work of art itself. To concentrate on what has been chipped away (the negative) is to ignore the whole purpose and reality of the positive creation.

—*What We Believe*

Above all, we desire transparent simplicity, for we want the glory to go to Him who has given us this "hope of glory, Christ in us." We wish to impress only our Husband. We desire what is precious in *His* sight, not what is precious in a fallen world's sight. To the world we desire only to present the true expression of Him in the purest of loves, not what would entice and seduce the world to Him.

—*Tolerance, Externalism and Holiness*

Col. 1:27

Single-Mindedness toward God

Simplicity governs our relationship to the world and the things of the world—it puts to death the lust of the flesh, the lust of the eyes and the pride of life that the tree of knowledge tempts us with. The world and its "ruler" have colonized not only our minds and hearts but also our bodies; and simplicity is a way to "decolonize" all three. To have true simplicity is thus to live in single-mindedness of heart toward God. It means that we are truly centered in God, are able to "buy as though [we do] not possess," and that we can "use this world as not misusing it." For we recognize that "the form [fashion] of this world is passing away."

Looking at it another, blunter way, we could picture the overflowing garbage dumps of the world metastasizing daily. These are full of the daily waste of human lives, the garbage of superfluous living—whether food, packaging, toys, empty beer cans and wine bottles, out-of-date record players, cassettes, old televisions, old computers, old books, newspapers, old appliances, old furniture, cars, transmissions, grease, oil or whatever. Overall, it represents the stench and wreckage of failed simplicity. Ironically, another name for hell is "Gehenna," which was the ever-burning garbage dump outside of Jerusalem.[1]

At the end of your life, when everything is separated and weighed out, will your life feel like an accumulation of garbage to be burned—full of garbage possessions no one even wants, garbage gadgets, garbage keepsakes, garbage desires, garbage lusts, garbage ambitions, garbage attitudes, garbage pride, garbage lies, garbage thoughts, garbage images, garbage character—or will you have sim-

---

Gen. 3:1-6; 1 John 2:16; John 12:31; 14:30; 16:11; 1 Cor. 7:30-31

plified your life by cutting out the garbage to leave standing only the image of Christ? Simplicity takes care of the garbage so that our lives don't *become* garbage.

—What Makes Your Church So Different?

Great and Wondrous Gifts

Two main positive rewards come to those who are received into the community of Christ. One, not only do you declare your exodus from the great conveyor belt of a meaningless life as it dumps droves of humanity into a dark and equally meaningless death, but you also can now *enjoy* the experience of a life full of meaning, a life that struggles to preserve and advance into the future a community that will be worth entering for the young and yet-to-be-born. This struggle is the redemptive experience of living in Christ's sacrifice by simply doing daily what's right and what has to be done.

Yours is the joy that comes when what you think, what you say and what you do all move in harmony with each other. And every time we old ones see one of you new members of the community take your stand against the wrong, fight for what's right or daily do what has to be done, no matter how great or small the task, it affirms to us that all the sacrifices that we and others before us have made—all in order to pass on this community to you and to the future—were worth the price, that *you* were worth our sacrifice because *what we have given* was worth something to you.

The second reward enjoyed by the members of Christ's community resides in *the life of the Spirit*—the spiritual gifts coming to us from cheerful men, women and children buoyed up by zest and humor, enthusiasm and camaraderie. This Spirit of life is felt and expressed to us in supernaturally powerful words of spoken truth, in the vibrant songs of community, in the self-sacrificing love-service of our people, in community crafts, skills, work, play and the other myriad activities of the community of life. It is symbolized in the ringing of the great bell that calls us to Sunday meetings or that rings out in celebration at weddings or in its solemn tolling of the knell for parting loved ones. It is embodied in the sounds of children laughing and playing at church picnics or around the old homestead, in joyous people dancing the horas at weddings and community celebrations, even the happy rattle and jingle of the traces of draft horses and mules as they plow through springtime fields, or in the spring-water fragrance of those freshly plowed fields, or in the smell of a corral full of horses and hay, or in the sound of cows lowing in the morning dew before milking time, or of chickens clucking as they settle on their roosts in the evening, or the covering of birdsong over all the land as we old ones sit on our porch swings in the fall and watch smiling neighbors strolling happily through the farm preparing for Thanksgiving and the Fair.

And out of this cheerfulness and joy comes the *gratitude* for great and wondrous gifts. And when you stop to think about it, all of it is quite a miracle for the day in which we live.

—Do You Really Mean It?

Work That Is Sacred

For us, homesteading skills and crafts take place in a plexus of relationships with creation, creatures and Creator that make them exceedingly meaningful—so meaningful, in fact, that they become sacred in the context of our sacralized life.

—*What We Believe*

Many people, of course, wonder what they are at their core, but I don't think the essence of what we are is ever so readily revealed as in the essentials of life: in feeding yourself by the labor of your own hands, in finding and fulfilling your true calling in life, in making the great decisions about marriage, in giving birth to new life, in trying to impart character to children by raising them and teaching them yourself, in coming to the moment of truth about your relationship with God and, finally, in the great travail of dying.

—*A Time of Harvest*

Imagine an occurrence as simple as when your seven-year-old son, whom your wife has just begun to teach at home, rushes into the living room after his first reading and says, "Dad, can I show you something?" He then clears his throat, holds back his head and carefully sounds out the words: "G-o-d is l-igh-t." Then he stands with sweet face beaming and dark eyes shining under a black shock of ragged bangs and you understand why you face the risks. "*Because we picked up responsibility for the living of life,*" you say to yourself, "this fruitfulness came forth, at least in part, through us." It's the same feeling when you sit down around your table with your family and say, "Kids, do you realize that everything on this table came from our own land by the labor of our own hands—that we are truly *living* off the land?" It is when we acknowledge the Giver of every good and perfect gift that we know with certainty that "*Laborare est orare*," that such "Labor is worship," that the Voice *can* sing within a people as well as through the land. Such work is sacred because the life it sustains is sacred—it is the best we can do consecrated to the highest we can know.

—*A Journey Home*

Choosing the Right Dreams

If we've had any success, it has been in lives and not money. This, more than anything, I want to pass on to my children and my children's children, that they should not forget what God brought us out of and the sacrifices and miracles that made possible the life they enjoy. It is good that we should know, in the words of one visitor, "how we came to all this."

Some have asked, "What have you learned from it all?" Well, along our portion of this great journey, we have learned that when your dreams start becoming a reality, they will cost you something—no, they will cost you everything, everything but your dreams. You cannot imagine that you will end the journey the same person that began it. That is why you must do better than your best to make sure your dream is more than good before you start. Some unchanging azimuth in your heart must tell you that your dream is life itself.

—A Journey Home

A Particular Culture

Culture consists of everything that people do. Human culture is the "total process of human activity and [the] total result of such activity."[2] Culture is the nurturing habitat that molds and shapes the people planted in its soil.

Scripture tells us that when God created the first man, He didn't simply set him adrift in space, leaving him without any place or direction for his life. God planted the man in a very specific physical culture and gave him clear directions about the path he should follow. God placed the man, in fact, in a garden, in an agricultural setting: "Yahweh God took the man and put him in the Garden of Eden to work it and take care of it" (Gen. 2:15). So God planted man in a particular culture, a particular nurturing habitat. God placed him in the setting in which He wanted him to live, giving him the work He wanted him to do. The man's spiritual destiny, God was declaring, would always be bound up in his relationship to the place where he was situated, the culture—the land. The very word for "man" in Hebrew, *adam*, compels recognition of this essential connection with earth and soil, *adamah*.

It is true that sin comes from within, that living in a rural setting can never redeem or save anyone. But the real question is whether seed can flourish in uncultivated ground and whether we are the planting of the Lord. If so, then there's little doubt that some cultures or "soils" are better than others for certain types of seed—bananas don't flourish in Alaska. And there's also little doubt about what kind of culture God has provided for us to flourish in.

—Culture, Agriculture and the Land

Ps. 51:5; Jer. 17:9; Rom. 7:17-20, 23-24; Isa. 28:24-26; 61:3; Matt. 13:19-23; 15:13; 1 Cor. 3:7-9; Heb. 6:7

Garden of God

For us, it is not a question of trying to live either in the past or in the future but in as close proximity as possible to the eternal: that is, we prefer those things of more enduring, permanent value.

—What We Believe

A God-centered culture is a covenant culture—a spiritual garden set off by walls or other lines that demarcate it as a special area of relationship and husbandry—through which the seed of God's Word is nurtured within our hearts until we come into perfect oneness with Him so that we may once again dwell with God in paradise.

A God-centered culture, then, is one that encourages the individual to conform himself to the image of God; this is because the corporate image of the community that rests upon that culture is conformed to the image of God. This image is the image of covenant; for covenant expresses God's nature—His faithful, eternal love—and thus true, godly culture is the culture of covenant. God's law-Word, which expresses the terms of His covenant, conforms us to a particular order of relationships, a way of life, a way of seeing, believing and behaving; and from that order, lifestyle and vision—that is, from our conformance to the covenant's terms—is formed the corporate image that God has ordained for His community.

We, in turn, enter into oneness with God by conforming ourselves to the image that He has ordained for us, both as individuals and as a community. Only by conforming our lives in every area to the pattern and way of life ordained by God can we enter into true oneness with our fellow

---

Rev. 2:7

man, with nature and with God Himself, for only this God-ordained culture fully expresses His covenant. And only through His covenant can we know Him. With His Word sown within us, and with us planted in His covenant community and culture, we can become once again the garden of God. We can grow into oneness with the God who is love. And this oneness with Him is our salvation.

—*A Garden Enclosed*

"A Garden Enclosed"

The Bible speaks of God's Word as seed. And it is the seed that carries within itself the genetic code, the information, that will determine the plant's appearance. Yet it is the *soil* that causes that seed to grow. Our covenant with God acknowledges that we have *freely* given Him, as the Husbandman, legitimate access to cultivate the garden of our lives. He has purchased us with a price and so can now "plant, weed, prune and fertilize" in order to bring forth the fruit of His Spirit, His very nature, in our lives.

The degree to which we live out the covenant determines the degree of access the Husbandman actually has into our lives to accomplish His purpose. It shows whether we have truly surrendered the title deed of our heart to its rightful owner and therefore whether we have genuinely authorized Him to cultivate our hearts—"a garden enclosed is my sister, my bride."

A community, if faithful to God's covenant, becomes the good soil husbanded to bring the seed of God's Word to maturity as fruit. When believers enter covenant, they agree to be informed within the context of that covenanted community. They desire more than an image merely pasted on the surface of their lives. They long, rather, to open themselves to the incorruptible seed of God's Word so that both their appearance and character can vitally serve to express the Word hidden deep within their hearts.

What people will become largely results from how they have been informed, what seed their particular form of covenant has allowed to enter into their hearts.

—Tolerance, Externalism and Holiness

Luke 8:11; Mark 4:14-15, 27-28; Isa. 61:11; Song of Sol. 4:12

Part II
Covenant Love

An Unfolding Love

Abide in Me, and I in you. As the branch cannot bear fruit of itself, unless it abides in the vine, neither can you, unless you abide in Me. As the Father loved Me, I also have loved you; abide in My love.

—John 15:4, 9

Love is not a brief sizzle and then a pop or two in the pan, but an *unfolding*, a process the dimensions of which cannot be experienced through fleeting dalliances. The love we seek fully reveals itself only when we take the way that leads to growth and unfolding development—it takes time for a tree to move from blossom time through the ripening time and then to fruit gathering time, when we finally taste its sweetness. So, too, the unfolding love of God comes through a growing, ever more intimate knowledge—a knowledge gained only in the simple but enduring pattern of unfolding relationship.

—Covenant Love

Chesed: The Daily Walk of Prose

Just as the wedding ceremony marks only the beginning of the actual marriage relationship, so our pledge of covenantal faithfulness to God marks only the beginning of our marriage to Him within the community of *His* design. The Hebrews had a special term to denote this *continuing* faithfulness to the covenant. This special term distinguished it from the initial vow to faithfulness and fidelity. The term was *chesed*.

Chesed shows that love is more than a few rare and dazzling flights of poetry—it is also the daily walk of prose. It is more than a dramatic, punctiliar act of faith—it is a *life* of fidelity, obedience and faithfulness. In the end the prose will better show love's strength, endurance and power to prevail in the details, intricacies and complexities of real-life relationships. So the poetry of love may reside in its moving profession, as in Ruth's words of covenant commitment to Naomi. But the prose lives out the profession, as in Ruth's gleaning from the fields, in her support of her mother-in-law and then in her marriage to Boaz. The poetry of love inspires us to value and then to make the covenant, the *b'rit*. But then the prose of love takes over in the lovingkindness, the care, the mercy, the fidelity, the determination and all the hard work that applies the b'rit to the duties of daily life.

So all this explains why to be a man or woman (or a God) of *chesed* is often translated in the Bible "*to be merciful*" —because to trust the one you stand in covenant with fills you with great peace and serenity—even great courage. So it's an act of mercy on someone's part to stand faithful to the covenant they have made. And such faithfulness can hardly help but fill you with great gratitude.

—Love That Works

Necessity of Covenant

Covenant brings all our romantic notions, gestures, fantasies and vague professions of love and care out of the ethereal realm of abstraction down to the real world of the concrete.

—Love That Works

Covenant, not sentimental or romantic notions, makes love real, makes it more than self-centered fantasy or animal lust endlessly perverted, as if constantly poking at it to spark some movement of life, like a cat tossing around a dead mouse, trying to prod it back to life so it can continue to play with it. Covenant, in contrast, offers the reality within which love is truly tested. As said, only in covenant can it be determined whether love is as powerful and wonderful as those who seek it have supposed it to be. Only through covenant can we prove whether it has the power to overcome and prevail in the everyday life of what is (often even without irony) called the "*real* world."

That is what *chesed* is: it is the durableness of love, love's enduring power over the duration of the fullness of our time on earth. And since all life faces unknowns that make us all vulnerable, covenant alone can cover the totality of life, even its unknowns. To enter covenant, then, means somehow finding the faith to totally trust not ultimately people but the God who puts people together to endure and prevail in love.

Form is not the content, but it is necessary in order to hold the content and then to channel it to meet human needs and all those purposes ordained by heaven. So the *fulfillment* of love vanishes apart from the *form* of the relationship, the form designed to hold the love.

—Love That Works

Self-Conquering Love

Real love conquers self first and then "conquers" the other not by seduction but by the magnitude of its sacrifice of self.

—Covenant Love

Love can only be seen as true when it can draw us outside of and beyond such radical, even pathological, individualism and into something greater than ourselves.

—What's the Problem with Love?

Of course, many no doubt can unknowingly experience and participate in God's love for many years. Yet, like Milton's proverbial pig feeding under the acorn tree, they never recognize and acknowledge the Source of that love. Instead, they glory in it themselves, as if it were self-generated. And so they first use, then abuse and finally destroy this love for their own selfish purposes. They only look up toward heaven when the acorns cease to fall, and that is usually only to shake their fist at the Source for not keeping the fodder flowing.

—*Leaving the Lonely Labyrinth*

To love and be loved is to sacrifice a certain independence in hopes of finding a balanced and mutual interdependence, which naturally turns us to some common outside source. In short, if true love exists at all, then its source must lie beyond us. It must, it seems, be a given, like life itself.

But inturning self-worship is not love. Outturning love plays havoc with the inturning human instincts for self-preservation, a word that tacitly points to fear as something positive and noble—fear of death and of self-loss. So those seeking to generate a truly self-defined love are as likely to succeed in their quest as an aging man might succeed in generating youth, immortality and eternal life from within his decaying and dying body. No matter how heroic his struggle, he eventually deteriorates and dies. So, too, does self-generated love seem to always grow stale and die. It even loses its ability to care whether it succeeds or not—it just shrivels into its little pod of self-preservation, cynicism, despair and the fear of death.

—What's the Problem with Love?

Life's Inevitable Tests

When people come to crises that require ultimate decisions, they grope for the old feelings but don't know why such feelings seem now to elude them. "Something has died in me," they often can be heard to complain. In actuality, real love simply required too great a burden and sacrifice for them, too great a humbling of their image of themselves. So their "love," no longer real, becomes a tool of their often increasingly frantic manipulation of circumstances and people for their own selfish purposes, a manipulation that becomes all the more frantic as they see the potential for love slipping irretrievably beyond their reach. Finally, they lose even the ability to any longer care whether love lives or dies in them and their relationships.

It is not, however, that their love was never real. Such love is not Shakespeare's weed but Shakespeare's flower turned sour by its deeds. It confronts the choice as to whether to believe that its love is God's gift or is instead self-generated, and therefore self-defined. And at that fateful moment of choice, it chooses self as the center (whether consciously or otherwise). Yet surely that weed that never laid claim to love seems in the end more wholesome and honest in its unpretentious lack of fragrance than the odor of the festering flower, the odor of a love corrupted and debased by selfish purposes while nonetheless still mouthing with foul breath the claim that its love is pure and selfless. Such root dishonesty and pride usually becomes impervious to real love. It shuts it out as "unreal" or, at best, as a less significant love.

—Leaving the Lonely Labyrinth

There will be times when, after we've pledged faithfulness to a covenant, it will take all the courage we have, and then some we don't yet have, to keep placing one foot in front of another, and keep walking faithfully in what we have pledged.

―*Love That Works*

The Harmony of Human Relationship

If the form of relationship is not given by God, then it hardly matters how much we feel. But what defines these emotions as love is whether we pour them into a form given by the God who is love and therefore who defines for us what is love.

—*Covenant Love*

For many, to even bring up the word *order* in regard to human relationships means bringing up vague connotations of a suspect authority exerted in social relationships and backed by coercive political power. Yet we write here from an entirely different perspective. As with many others throughout history, for us, both order and authority have come to carry different, non-coercive connotations.

For instance, the word *order* actually derives from the same Indo-European root as the word *art*. It means "to *fit* together." This implies a contrast to either an anarchical disorder or a coercive order that *forces* together. Originally, the word *order* began its long and varied life by being used to designate a row of threads on a loom. From the same root of *art* and *order*, the Greek word *harmos*, comes the carpenter's word for *joinery* and also the word for *harmony*. So the concept of people freely coming together in good will, in community, can presumably take on the connotations of an art, and the order of human relationships can become the carpenter's craft of joinery, the weaver's craft of warping and wefting, the composer's craft of harmonics in music.

Put this together with the Latin meaning of the root word for *authority*, *auctor*, which means "creator," and the end result makes the alternative kingdom of love more like a song than a chain of command.

—What Kind of Family?

Life Inheres within the Form

We stand with those who believe something special and unique exists between a man and wife, between parents and children, something that cannot be experienced apart from the *given order* that joins them together in a certain form of relationship, any more than a hand can experience life if severed from the body, or if grotesquely sutured to its own "favorite," self-invented and "redesigned" place, say, on the forehead or between the eyes. Just as in the case of the human body, the family (and even any community based on the notion of givens, of destiny) is simply not subject to radical redefinition and reordering, at least not without destroying its very structure as a "given," a given that allows another unmanufactured given—life—to continue unfolding.

When you destroy the *given* order of the family, you, in short, destroy both the life and the family. An apple tree chainsawed to the ground and then stacked next to the wall as cordwood hardly remains an apple tree, or any sort of tree for that matter. This is true even though its constituent parts might still exist in their basically original form, except, of course, for their dissection and dislocation from all the rest and the fact that it will never again bear what gave it its identity—apples.

Or take another, more gruesome example: upon entering a room that has a human leg lying on a chair, another in the closet, a torso behind the couch, two arms against the wall and a head over by the stairwell, no one would say that they "just met the nicest person" in that room: the person is no longer there. Life inheres in the wholeness of the precise *form*—the "fixed order"—of relationships that the parts assume. And so if you destroy the form, the order, you destroy the life. With, then, a reinvented family, you can pretend that what you then have is still a family, but just because you choose to call a copperhead a cottontail and you exult in your freedom to do so, it doesn't turn serpents into rabbits.

—What Kind of Family?

We Love That Which We Trust

Finding the right kinds of relationships of deep and positive emotions with those who will really care for and about us—and fulfilling new roles in those relationships—is absolutely crucial in shaping who we are, and who those around us will be. This proves true on the very deepest levels of our lives. This reflects how deeply emotion and belief are intrinsically related—that we feel the most about whom or what we *believe* in or *trust* the most.[3]

Here, then, at least at first, seems to be one key for understanding the working of love: if you want to deeply love someone, then find someone fully trustworthy; if you want to be loved, then prove yourself fully trustworthy, according to the form of relationship you are agreeing to.

—What's the Problem with Love?

"Until Death Do Us Part"

When God established the covenant of marriage, He never promised that we would have no hard times, no trials, no troubles, no pain, no adjustments, no sorrows, no failures, no tragedies, no disappointments. The love we are speaking of is not a fantasy that removes us from the struggle of having to live in a lapsed world rife with cruelty, pain, disease, suffering and death—rather, it is a grace that strengthens us in such a way so that supernatural love prevails in all those life struggles. God, then, was merely proving through the marriage covenant that love is in truth powerful enough to triumph over every obstacle. At least this is true for those who commit themselves, through the sacred vow of covenant, to walk steadfastly in this covenantal path. So when two people enter into the marriage covenant, they vow before God to commit themselves to walk love's path together "until death do us part." If in truth they have been joined together by God's perfect will, then the injunction from heaven declares: "What *God* has joined together, let no *man* put asunder."

—Committed to Love

An Enduring Sense of Awe

This feeling of the most profound seriousness in the face of such life-determining choices is what has filled so many people over the centuries with such an overwhelming sense of awe on the day they step to the altar to sacralize their decision to marry.

—Committed to Love

If the lover and beloved hold *two different views* of what constitutes the one love that is to hold them together, then they begin with an almost insurmountable obstacle, at least if their desire really is to establish a relationship that can bring genuine oneness or union. Even their ideas of what constitutes love are not one. How, then, can they be united when they remain at odds in understanding what constitutes the most basic phenomenon—love—that supposedly will bring this union? We can call the love that allows two people to come together "tolerance," but it has never been the mere "tolerance" of one musical instrument for the other that creates a symphonic orchestra, an orchestrated whole that makes beautiful music *together*.

This helps explain why continual compromise of what each believes, sees, values and feels often merely bleeds the relationship into a weak and enervated anemia. It may only produce self-congratulatory but intellectually and emotionally sterile, even insipid and vacuous, individuals who can never sound the depths of each other's lives as two mysteriously *different* human beings. Such a life of compromise often only produces a diluted "love," one with no vitality, no passion, no meaning, no purpose and no power.

Neither has this shown much success in fulfilling or even holding together relationships, and after these compromises have done their bloodletting work to leech off the pressure, whatever remains that seems worth salvaging or preserving can be collected in a bucket and carried to court. Even in the best of relationships, often only a sustained tension of wills remains, even if we try to dignify it by still calling it a "relationship," a relationship now attended to with lots of superficial smiles geared to show how "unaffected" we are by someone who has just ripped the fabric of our life apart and torn us to the quick.

—What's the Problem with Love?

Transcendent Faith for the Journey

To stop loving each other before death is to join the despairing dropouts along the ditches that mark both sides of the way of pilgrimage. It is to give up on the vision of the new land—the land of human beings redeemed by love. It is, in short, to have allowed yourself to accept that such love was merely an illusion, when all along it was only your own ideas of love and the desacralized context you tried to plant love in that were illusory. But to accept that love has failed you merely because your illusions have failed love will shatter one of the most profound and precious hopes and experiences of human life.

It scarcely needs saying, then, that the tremendous journey that constitutes a marriage requires a faith far beyond what most people today, situated in their utterly secular worlds, think of as normal. For only those who can truly hear the unseen Voice, the Voice that speaks from the all-seeing mountaintop, can find the faith, the courage, the integrity to take even the first step of pilgrimage in the full light of all its possible but yet unknown implications.

If this Voice can no longer be heard, if there is no garden of God, no sacred community in which such a love can be planted and nurtured, if people can no longer make the pilgrimage to the peak of the mountain, then experiencing a deep, enduring and fulfilling love would also appear to be impossible. Yet despite all the unknowns that envelop the marriage commitment, an overwhelming feeling continues to resound in human hearts, bringing many a soul to the profound moment of awe at the prospect of their marriage to another human being. Many, in other words, would still declare that something transcendent to petty desires, fantasies or selfish ambitions has profoundly moved their hearts toward a marriage that will last a lifetime.

—*Committed to Love*

Stepping into the Unknown

Entering covenant requires a deliberate step into the unknown. Our commitment would never take us to this "*new*" land" unless we had first launched it on those *unknown* seas and sailed on even through the storms and into the unknowns of another's life and the unknowns of life itself. The willingness to keep our course in spite of life's intermittent and sometimes violent storms, as well as all of life's unknowns, constitutes faith, the fidelity to love, to its source in God and to the form that holds love's content. It is a faith that believes love will never fail, that it will always prevail.

None of this denies that to open ourselves so completely to God requires the supreme act of trust, of faith. So on some level we realize that we do *not* now know Him as we could or will know Him. To commit ourselves to becoming completely vulnerable to God, then, requires a deliberate step into our insufficient knowing—into, that is, the unknown. *Every* marriage begins with such a step—whenever anyone enters into such a covenant, that person enters with the purpose of coming to know what is unknown, not only about the other but about themselves as well. This is done with the conscious understanding that such knowledge will come through a relationship of growing oneness.

To commit ourselves to become fully one with someone therefore means to commit ourselves to a path of ever-increasing knowledge of the unknown otherness of that person. This is knowledge of a particular type, a certain kind of relational, personal knowledge, in contrast to merely detached, impersonal information about someone. This knowledge will enter the unknown but enduring substance of another's very being and thus begin to reveal a portion of the mystery of the other's essence and, again, of our own as well, and so also of love and life.

Such a covenant will, of course, also expose our lovelessness; but, by doing so, it presents us with the opportunity to slough off that lovelessness, believing that something else—a great and overcoming power called *"agape,"* God's own love—will in the end enter us in response to our cries for help in this often painful enlargement of our inner selves, that it will rescue us from our isolate and narrow selfishness, even settle down in us to abide and rule at the center of our lives.

—*Committed to Love*

Complementarity

It is indeed a profound mystery that two different worlds can coalesce to create another world, which unites with yet another world, which creates yet another—all ordered and directed by God. And all this occurs, from one generation to the next, without destroying what has been legitimately passed on from the past. This is what Abraham started and why he did "not receive what was promised" so that he would "not be made perfect" or complete "without us." So each generation only further develops and expands what preceded it. Each carries forward the original seeds of purpose, causing them to grow and press on to new levels of growth and fulfillment, levels never fully attained before. And this is something that can only come through those *differences*, those *complementarities*, commingled in God's own Spirit through a series of spiritual rebirths that reach ever higher toward the image of God. Again, it is the differences, then, that have the potential to create a new, but not *entirely* new, expression of the old family and all its great truths.

The distinction between male and female serves as a means to offset this human proclivity toward self-exaltation, for it makes unmistakably clear that, from this viewpoint, none of us can be complete in himself or herself, but that we are all mutually dependent creatures rather than independent little divinities. This mutual dependence is expressed in the complementarity of "the male and female components of the one 'man,'" with each of the genders "inherently created in unity," albeit a "unity" only possible within the order specified by God's Word.[4]

Within the context of this order, "one is not better than the

---

Heb. 11:8, 13, 39-40

other; or less human, or less potentially divine. When Paul in Galatians 3:28 wrote, 'there is neither male nor female,' he was expressing this truth in another way,"[5] though we cannot ignore the context in which he affirmed this denial, that there is "neither male nor female" only when both are "*in* Christ," which implies an order of its own—the order that constitutes the Body of Christ as indicated in 1 Corinthians 11 through 12. This complementarity and mutual dependence serve both to humble each of us and also to point the relationship of man to woman in marriage ("the two shall become one") toward a relationship in Christ that transcends their humanity alone, as Paul explicitly states in Ephesians 5.

So both gender and familial complementarity point toward a still greater complementarity—that of humanity united with deity as it was in the incarnation, "in Christ." All this suggests that in some sense, in the Biblical view, marriage was to direct people toward the transcendent.

—Committed to Love

Union between God and His People

For as a young man marries a virgin, so shall your sons marry you; and as the bridegroom rejoices over the bride, so shall your God rejoice over you.

—Isaiah 62:4-5

Husbands, love your wives, just as Christ also loved the church and gave Himself for her.

—Ephesians 5:25

The Judaic view of marriage represented something even more awesome than the joining of the two different worlds of husband and wife: in its highest form, it represented the joining of humanity to the ultimate Other—God. It therefore symbolized the union between God Himself and a people. This was made explicit in the Old Testament but also became a major theme of the New Testament in the relationship between Messiah, the Bridegroom, and the church, the Bride.

In fact, our ultimate, and even preeminent, interest here is not earthly marriage but, rather, this love covenant between God and humankind, a covenant that situates human marriage meaningfully in God. Though, of course, a difference in degree between the earthly and the heavenly covenant is apparent, nonetheless—in at least one sense—both covenants illustrate, or at least both *should*, the same type of love and the same type of relationship; and Scripture plainly teaches this.

It is for this type of love that God readily risked everything in order to enter a covenant with humankind in a perpetual and everlasting vow taken in His own name. So

---

Isa. 54:5-8; 62:3-5; Jer. 3:14-15; Ezek. 16:1-14; John 3:28-29; Eph. 5:22-32; 2 Cor. 11:2, KJV; Rev. 21:2-3, 8-10; Gen. 22:15-18; Heb. 6:13-15

the transcendent God of heaven stands ready to join hand in nail-pierced hand with lowly people in a supernal marriage ceremony that says, "Place your right hand, the very sign of your own authority over your own life, into My right hand, into My authority, and touch there the piercing evidence of the covenant commitment that bound Me to you at the cross, in love's ultimate triumph over death."

—*Committed to Love*

Possessed by Love

Many never experience ecstasy in love because they flee from the agony of total self-surrender. So, whether in marriage, in birth, in child rearing, in their calling, in their religious life or in their death, they refuse to give themselves completely enough that they may be said to finally "stand outside" themselves (the literal meaning of *ecstasy*), to be possessed completely by love. Yet, no matter how frightening it may seem, how can you possibly even hope to "stand outside yourself" unless you are first willing to *totally* surrender yourself?

The Biblical view presents holiness as nothing less than this total self-surrender to God in love. And such a surrender only results from what Søren Kierkegaard called an "infinite passion,"[6] as distinct from finite passions, such as lusts, infatuations, desires, ambitions, rivalries, competition, envy, covetousness and the like. When a bride totally surrenders herself to her husband, until even her identity is absorbed into his, and a husband gives all that he is for his bride, only then do we begin to get some idea of the reaches of ecstasy that the word held for some people in the past.

Likewise parents, when truly fulfilling their responsibilities as parents, *belong* to their children *because of the parents'* love for their children—not because the *children* have externally placed and enforced certain demands upon parents. The value the parents place on their children's lives lend the latter an aura of awe in the parents' eyes. Because of this love and appreciation—that is, because the children are precious, and of the highest possible value to the parents—such parents long to see them fulfilled, long to see them as happy as they can conceivably be in the deepest sense of blessedness. So whatever the parents *can* do to bring this to pass they also feel an *inward* compulsion to do.

In short, the children *possess* the parents' time, their thoughts, their affections, their resources, not because of any coercive demands forced upon the parents, but because of the magnitude of *parental* love for their children. The parents *cannot stop* loving, caring, relating to them; and because they cannot, they truly belong to their children— they are their children's (possessive case) parents.

—*What Kind of Family?*

Agony unto Ecstasy

So *agape* is not the love of exploitation, nor of social condescension: it is love that takes a person outside of him- or herself; it is the ecstatic union of two subjects in which each pours himself out completely to God and thereby finds the common meeting place of perfect oneness in God as both parties bind themselves in covenant union first to Him and thereby to one another. When human relationships, such as with marriage or the relationship between parents and children, are centered in God, only then can they express such *agape* love. Otherwise, they can at best only participate in a human-centered *phileo* love. Only such a selfless love, a sustained *agape*, can meet the deepest human needs. Every other love offers merely superficial or temporary respite and only of transient or fleeting comfort.

—Leaving the Lonely Labyrinth

Love can only reside in a relationship that causes us to turn *away* from self-love and *toward* someone other than ourselves. It seems, then, that love involves both an agony and an ecstasy—that is, only the agony of unreserved self-surrender can even hope to find the fullest ecstasy of a lasting love. Again, Jesus' entire life taught this truth—so He didn't preserve His life but gave it away, gave it for love in the agony of the cross and received love's reply in the resurrection.

—What's the Problem with Love?

The Greatest Witness

When the rule of love truly takes charge, no one man or woman is ever in control. Rather, the Spirit is understood by all as the source of "control" for everything and everyone in the covenantal context of God-given relationships. Then community life becomes like an intricate mosaic, with each one working on a particular area until all the "pieces" fit perfectly together, even though no one seemed to plan it that way. Only if there is a God who has arranged human lives in love, and who is directly active in human affairs, can such a society exist. So such a community of people living in such oneness becomes the greatest witness to the existence and active concern of God in human affairs.

God will only fully enter human relationships and bring that kind of harmony, however, when people cease to live only for themselves. When a selfless and caring attitude prevails, when Jesus' love truly and fully motivates people, this releases everyone to not only want to do their best but also to actually begin to do it, since they will be filled with joy in the experience, joy in the powerful presence of the God who is love as He works in and through them by His resonant Spirit.

No continuous surveillance over such a people proves either desirable or necessary, since they have a highly attuned and sensitized conscience, a conscience covenantally committed to pleasing God by doing only His will and not their own. When no one concentrates on self-seeking rewards or personal "empowerment" or self-validating or -aggrandizing images but on the empowerment only possible when all collaborate in the self-sacrificing love

Eph. 3:14-19; John 17:20-23; 13:34-35

and service of Christ, then their work, whether in crafts or farming or business or teaching or child rearing or home management or prophetic visioning, truly becomes a love-service to God and to others. It is never then "*my*" accomplishment but "our" accomplishment *in God*.

This means that a return to any of the traditional vocations and other patterns of traditional community life would first necessarily be preceded by a return to traditional relationships given and ordered by God. If these relationships come first, then a return to traditional vocations and ways of life in traditional community also brings a release of each individual to exercise his or her gifts responsibly in true liberty.

—What Kind of Family?

Love Is as Strong as Death

A special significance attaches to the permanence of the marriage covenant. This enduring quality of covenant serves to show humanity the unconquerable durability of *agape*. Only *God's* love could ever hold a marriage together in a way that brings continually growing oneness and fulfillment. Fill in between the lines of this thought, and the conclusion is that the marriage covenant can serve to reveal God's love as the most potent, enduring power in the universe. We can only, of course, reasonably accept this as truth if, as Scripture declares, God Himself is love. Paul speaks of this enduring power in 1 Corinthians 13:8 when he says that "love never fails." The scriptural love song, the Song of Solomon, also expresses this same view of the power of covenant love when it declares: "Love is as strong as death; many waters cannot quench love."

—Committed to Love

---

1 John 4:8, 16

Love Binds Together

In contrast to the power of dissolution and death, love expresses the power of cohesion, the power that holds together, the power that alone can end fragmentation and dissolution and draw all reality into oneness and harmony. In short, the binding covenant of sacrificial, redemptive love is precisely what starts the process that *ends* the curse of dissolution.

The book of Hebrews speaks of Jesus as "the radiance of God's glory and the exact representation of His being," the full manifestation of the God who "*is* love." Paul also declared that "in Him all things *hold together*." Love is the power that brings oneness, coherence, harmony. Paul further described love as the sacred "*bond* of peace." It *binds* together. The covenant love of God has power enough to even conquer the dissolution inherent in the curse of death.

The power of this love was manifested in the life of Jesus Christ, who gave "all the substance of His house for love." His body went down to death, but it rose again "because it was impossible for death to keep its hold on Him." It was impossible because He lived a life conceived by the eternal Spirit of love, because He then lived a life in perfect covenantal conformity to that love. So death *could not hold Him*: it could not bind Him to or in its dissolution. His covenant bond with God and life proved stronger.

It is this all-conquering covenant love—a love originating *only* in God Himself—of which Paul spoke when he said: "But in all these things we overwhelmingly *conquer*

Col. 3:14; 1:17; Heb. 1:3; Eph. 4:3; Song of Sol. 8:6-7; Acts 2:24; Matt. 1:18-23; John 14:9-11

through Him who *loved* us. For I am convinced that neither *death*, nor life, nor angels, nor principalities, nor things present, nor things to come, nor powers, nor height, nor depth, nor any other created thing, shall be able to *separate us* from the *love* of God" (Rom. 8:37-39).

—*Committed to Love*

The Power and Peril of Love

A force so powerful as love—one that can conquer even death and that represents the rule of a kingdom entirely counterposed to a lapsed world's—cannot become a plaything of human self-indulgence. Such a love is no more a game than the death it ultimately conquers. And we can see how a force so powerful could weld souls together as one, to be separated only with unspeakable anguish and pain because of the self-centeredness of one of the parties involved. To play with such a force is like a child playing with fire. The fire, of course, fascinates the child, but it also holds more power and peril than most children can imagine. To childishly play with such a love has not only seared tenderness and trust in human hearts, which happens when the innocent emotions of love and joy are burnt out and become the ashes of bitterness and resentment, but playing with this fire has also brought untold damage to the human soul and spirit as well. And for many, it does all this irremediably.

—*Committed to Love*

Protection Provided through Covenant

Everyone wants to be loved for what they perceive as their true self and not merely for something that each only pretends or appears to be on the surface, or something that they know is temporary and passing. Without such a love, each remains cut off and isolated in his or her most essential being, fragmented and sundered from all other life. This decomposition at the center, this isolation at the core, is a precursor to the experience, the sorrow, the profound loneliness and despair, that always seem to lie waiting up ahead somewhere in a meaningless death.

This is the pain that the Biblical God is portrayed as seeing in souls everywhere. It is said to have so moved Him to compassion that He exposed Himself to unspeakable violation in order to come to us where we are, to tell us that we are not alone in our suffering but that there is a secret place of abiding and protected relationships that the human soul longing for love may call home.

—Committed to Love

Vulnerability within the Protection of Covenant

It is God who must ultimately teach us that we can only disclose this secret self—this person we truly are—within the covenant that He Himself has given. For we surely know that such a disclosure of ourselves makes us vulnerable to deep inner injury, and only a sacred and serious covenant offers protection in such vulnerability. But this covenant has to work *both* ways.

So to enter into covenant with God means to no longer hide our naked souls from His presence and truth. Marriage to Him means laying bare the soul before Him and covering nothing from Him. We make ourselves totally vulnerable to Him *in* our covenant. We expose our inner selves to the searching light of His Word.

The covenant covers and protects so long as we faithfully abide within its garden walls. Within those protective walls of the covenant, we can open our hearts to God without fear at our exposure; for we know that we have entered into a place that will ultimately bring to completeness our union with God.

Outside of this covenant, such exposure, such nakedness, constitutes a sort of spiritual exhibitionism, flaunting itself in flirtation, seduction, fornication, adultery, prostitution—an *indecent* exposure on one level or another. Inside the walls of covenant, however, no one need suffer Adam's shame before their heavenly Husband. They can make their innermost, secret self vulnerable within the covenant because their love—their oneness with

---

John 3:21, Ampl.; Heb. 4:12-13; Matt. 10:26-27; Eph. 5:12-14; 1 Cor. 14:24-25; Rom. 2:16; Rev. 2:23; Jer. 17:9-10

God—"covers a multitude of sins" (1 Pet. 4:8). Only by readily opening ourselves to this degree, by making ourselves completely vulnerable to God, can we begin to truly come into oneness with Him.

—Committed to Love

Mutual love given in covenant commitment becomes a great source of courage. The knowledge of such a love's sure and unfailing steadfastness brings the courage to open our hearts and make known our own deepest needs, even as we take responsibility for serving the needs of others. Such a life dedicated to love really offers no alternative to vulnerability.

—Building Christian Character

The Humility of Love

Love suffers long and is kind; love does not envy; love does not parade itself, is not puffed up.

—*1 Corinthians 13:4*

In the Biblical view, the sole passageway to love rooted in the transcendent God lies in the most difficult of acts for fallen human beings—the total and complete acknowledgment that, as the apostles Paul and James, as well as Jesus, declared, *nothing within us* can be credited as the source of love and goodness. So this way demands the absolute humbling and abasing of ourselves before the Creator who is love. This humbling must provoke, by God's grace, a deep longing for an ongoing change that gradually conforms us to *God's* image.

—*Leaving the Lonely Labyrinth*

Those who recognize the path they must follow to find true love must come to recognize that love lies outside themselves. They must come to see that love requires something from those who long for it—it calls on them to conform to this love's standards rather than try to make love conform to their own personal, self-made standards. Perhaps, then, the most difficult part of the great initial step toward love is that it can only begin with so radical a humbling before God that it constitutes a death to our old narcissistic way of understanding, of seeing, of living in the world; and this is followed by a transforming encounter with God so radical that it constitutes the spiritual experience not of a

---

Ps. 53:3; 34:18; 51:17; 1 John 4:8-10, 16; Matt. 19:17; 23:11-12; 18:4; Rom. 3:10, 12, 23; 5:5; 7:14-24; 8:29; 12:1-2; Jer. 17:9; James 1:17; 3:14-17; 4:6-10; 1 Cor. 13:4-8, 13; 2 Chron. 7:14; Prov. 3:34; Isa. 57:15; 66:2; 1 Pet. 5:5; Phil. 2:1-8

theoretical or theological rebirth but of an actual, tangible and supernaturally powerful rebirth.

—*What's the Problem with Love?*

The River of Love

Love is still here, will always be there, surging down the center of God's purpose, sustaining us all in different ways—in prayers, in the transferring of itself to, and the building of itself up in, the young and strong who now more and more must man the oars and sails of the coursing ship. They are now the ones who must carry on the vision and fulfill its burden of love by bearing it on into the future. None of that love has, however, departed. This river of love is just growing stronger and bigger and wider and broader and deeper as more and more tributaries rush in to join it. Then one day, we'll all reach the full measure of the stature of Christ, knowing the depth and the breadth and the width and the height of the love of God that He has poured out upon us. And that's what is taking place in these difficult, changing times.

—The Church in the Time of Lawlessness

Part III
Christian Character

The Meaning of "Character"

We also glory in tribulations, knowing that tribulation produces perseverance; and perseverance, character; and character, hope. Now hope does not disappoint, because the love of God has been poured out in our hearts by the Holy Spirit who was given to us.

—Romans 5:3-5

Hebrews 1:3 says that Jesus Christ is the "express image" or the "exact representation" of God's very Being. The words in quotation marks translate the Greek word *charakter*—the obvious source of our word *character*. When the minter of currency stamped an image on a coin, transferring an impression to it, the Greeks used this same word to describe the process. Character, in other words, is something *impressed* upon us, stamped into our inner nature by the weightiness of the burdens and responsibilities of life, as well as by the weightiness of honor that comes from our love and respect for God and for those over us in God.

—*Forming Christ's Body, Book One*

Knowledge or Love?

Knowledge puffs up while love builds up. Those who think they know something do not yet know as they ought to know.

—1 Corinthians 8:1-3

While parents and pastors should encourage those under their care to excel in all they do, the Bible warns against a kind of knowledge that puffs people up. True knowledge, Christ-centered knowledge, does not puff us up but nurtures humility as it brings us to recognize our complete dependence on the Giver of all true wisdom and, indeed, of every perfect gift. Such knowledge builds us up in love, and such an attitude enables our charges to live lives authentically guided by God's Spirit, worshiping Him all their days in both Spirit and Truth. All believers, young or old, must find God's forge of character and walk through the coals. If we succeed in everything else but fail here, then we have failed God, our children and God's flock. If we succeed in this area, then we can succeed in every area of child rearing or pastoral care.

—Building Christian Character

Honor versus Dishonor

Dishonor stands as one of the straightest roads to perdition and apostasy. But its opposite, honor, is the foundation from which all other elements of Christian character arise. It refers primarily to a condition of the heart and mind, an inner attitude that inevitably manifests itself in outer words, actions and demeanor. Honor expresses genuine and deep veneration.

When Peter describes the stone as *precious* to those who believe, he uses the Greek word *timē*, here translated as *precious*, which also means *honor*. It is the very word Jesus had used when declaring that a prophet is without honor in his hometown. This stone *is* precious. It *is* honored.

—Building Christian Character

Honesty

Perhaps the greatest means of honoring or respecting someone is honesty and openness with them. When we are honest, in other words, we stand open and exposed before others because we trust them. Honest people don't hide in darkness or try to escape the light; they walk transparently without pretense. And because they trust God, they trust those with whom God has brought them into covenant relationship.

—Building Christian Character

To keep our consciences pure, we must have the honesty to walk in the light as He is in the light. Only then will we be able to hear His voice and walk together with all the sheep of His flock. If we are dishonest and put away a good conscience, we cannot help but shipwreck in the faith.

The key in all this is the *attitude* we cultivate. Even if our works will never be fully perfect, will we strive, as Jesus commanded, to be perfect as our heavenly Father is? Will we allow Him to perfect our attitude and will in relationship to Him and to our brothers?

—Acknowledging God's Word

---

1 John 1:7; 1 Tim. 1:19; Matt. 5:48; Phil. 2:1-4

Discipline

A child only learns "the fear of the Lord" by learning to fear doing evil because he knows it results in discipline. The fear of the Lord is to "depart from evil." Therefore, to punish a child for wrongdoing not only teaches but *trains* him to "depart from evil" and thereby establishes the child in the fear of the Lord, that is, "in the way he should go." Parents cannot simply pray for this and then sit back, passively hoping that God will somehow make their children revere Him, counting on others to step in and do what they've failed to do.

The Bible speaks much of the supernatural and miraculous but speaks nothing positive about the realm of magic. Rather, God works "in *us* to *will* and to *do*." Yes, God works "*in us*," but *we* still must "*will* and *do*" according to the work of His Spirit and grace. According to the Bible, we have an active role in seeing "the fear of the Lord" rooted in our children's lives.

—*Building Christian Character*

Prov. 3:7; 22:6

The Fear of the Lord

The fear of the Lord is to hate evil, pride and arrogance and the evil way.

—Proverbs 8:13

Therefore, the fear of Yahweh, which "has to do with punishment" for wrongdoing, gives us the hearing ear of a "wise son," a hearing that brings us into perfect obedience and perfect love. This love stands as the *end* of wisdom. But where we fall short, we must "begin" again to both hear and obey by loving God's discipline and the "fear of the Lord" it brings.

The foundation of discipline doesn't lie in teaching masses of isolated rules and regulations, although children need a clear pattern of conduct. Rather, we can lay such a foundation by teaching children to respect godly authority and to promptly obey their parents as well as all those who express God's non-coercive authority. That is, they must come into proper *relationship* to God-given authority expressing the lordship of love.

To impart this knowledge—the knowledge that obedience to and honor of godly authority constitutes the most basic ethical imperative of their lives—becomes the first stage in discipleship. So this also constitutes the *primary* goal of child-rearing, and the Bible straightforwardly admonishes not only the use of corporal discipline to drive folly away from a child but also its use to instill the first step in developing wisdom, that is, knowledge.

—Building Christian Character

Prov. 13:1; 10:13; 26:3; 22:15

If someone you love is too proud to humble themselves before God, then pray that God will release His providential dealings to disintegrate the bonds of their pride, to help them find joy in humbling themselves, to give them a revulsion for what binds them, to turn their heart fully toward God, to soften their hard hearts and open their closed minds. Then pray that He'll give you the wisdom and the love to speak to them what they need to hear.

—Is Grandpa Saved?

Hearing and Obeying

Blessed are those who hear the word of God and obey it.

—Luke 11:28

Hearing is the obvious prerequisite of obeying: you must hear to obey. Indeed, the word in the Greek New Testament, *hupakouo*, generally translated as "obey," means literally "to come under the hearing of." By instilling the characteristics of godly fear, humility and honor, parents can teach the child sensitivity to the parental voice and will, with the ultimate goal being the child's sensitivity to the voice and will of God.

To hear requires silence. No one can obey unless they hear; and no one can hear unless they listen; and without listening, they cannot consistently speak what God would have them to speak.

—Building Christian Character

Dangers of Pride

Pride goes before destruction, and a haughty spirit before a fall.

—Proverbs 16:18

My own experience over the decades has led me to believe that almost every failure in the kingdom of God can ultimately be traced to a failure of humility and a triumph of pride, whether overt or subtle. The deceptions of pride are always obvious to those who observe it from the outside but almost never to those held captive within it.

—Building Christian Character

Pride kills. It kills as the door of the human heart slams tightly shut against every human face that would express God's love and noncoercive authority. Pride closes every avenue, every opening, every covenant channel through which that love moves and calls. God's love continues to seek a human soul until the door of pride finally bolts forever against love. Those centered in the arrogance of self imprison themselves in their own small universe. In their own narrow little world, self reigns as its own god, determines its own truth and destiny, while proudly answering to no one else.

—Leaving the Lonely Labyrinth

We can't cavalierly shoulder our way through life assuming we know everything, mainly because we certainly don't, and can't. Only the smugness and complacency of an arrogant pride, which more than anything blinds us to the truths hidden in the mystery of life, convinces us that we know everything we need to know in order to successfully and fully live life. But life has a way of showing us that it's much bigger not only than we thought but also bigger than we ever imagined.

—*Love That Works*

Self: Survival or Sacrifice?

For whoever desires to save his life will lose it, but whoever loses his life for My sake will find it.

—Matthew 16:25

Pride is the mechanism of a self-view that must rely on self-preservation at all costs, while humility is the mechanism of a view that can surrender self entirely to God's rule of *agape*. "Survival at all costs" or "Sacrifice the full cost"—these ultimately pose the only two real options. We can pretend, when we stand *outside* our confrontations with the inevitable crises of life, that we have more subtle choices that fall into shades of gray. But when those crises become ultimate, we will have only two—until we finally have none at all.

—*Nonviolence*

Luke 9:23-27; 14:26-33; Rom. 12:1-3; 1 Pet. 2:5

The True Nature of Humility

Let nothing be done through selfish ambition or conceit, but in lowliness of mind let each esteem others better than himself.

—Philippians 2:3

The humble person assesses himself with the sober measure of God's judgment and leans on the Lord with all his heart. God's strength is then made perfect through the weakness of the humble. Not thinking of himself more highly than he ought, but with gratitude in his heart for any gifts and talents God has given him, the humble person serves these to his brothers in God's stead, recognizing the privilege that God has given him. Humility is not thinking evil of oneself; it is giving no thought for oneself at all, while still recognizing one's limitations and obligations. Neither is it an affectation, such as the softening of one's face and laying back of one's ears, like a whipped dog.

It is a genuinely submissive attitude of the heart manifested in words and deeds. Nor is it thinking hatefully of oneself, which means you cannot then love others. It is rather thinking so much of God and the needs and worth of others that little remains to think of oneself at all.

When we truly walk in humility before God, we will esteem others higher than ourselves, knowing that only the grace of God makes us able to stand responsibly before Him. Because we have a true realization of what we are in the flesh, we can sincerely appreciate the mercy God extends to us when He allows us to participate in His kingdom. Yet at the same time, in our hearts we will recognize the gift

---

2 Cor. 12:9; Rom. 12:3; Matt. 22:37-40

that each and every one of our brothers and sisters is in Christ. We will see them as the precious souls for whom Jesus suffered and died. We will then earnestly seek every opportunity to serve them with all our hearts in their time of need.

—Building Christian Character

Humility Blossoms into Peace

Our dependence on God allows Him to sustain us in every circumstance and way. We trust in His abiding provision, whether it comes directly by His Spirit or through our brothers and sisters. So the increasingly dominant desire of our life is to fulfill God's will; and when we humbly and trustingly stand in the place of His perfect way, we know an equally perfect peace because our minds are stayed on Him.

—*Building Christian Character*

True humility reveals itself in true brokenness, and true brokenness only fully comes with a true and complete commitment to *fully* and utterly "submit . . . to God."

—*Bedrock*

Humility blossoms into peace in our lives because we no longer strive for position or eminence or to validate ourselves or our gifts to others. In short, those seeking to prove *themselves* are headed toward the terrible snare of strife, competition, self-validation and self-exaltation. There is a vast difference between the pride of *proving oneself* and the humility that alone can make full *proof of our ministry*. In regard to the former, our fellowship and relationship with God more than fulfills every need. So we don't measure ourselves among ourselves but find true security and fulfillment in a Christ-centered life of love.

—*Building Christian Character*

Pride's Emptiness

Pride is always empty—it has no substance beyond superficial and vain pretentiousness and conceit. It isn't nearly as heavy and weighty a thing as some people who inflate their own deeds and images believe. Pride blows away like a tumbleweed with every errant breeze. But a heart heavy with the honor, the love, the care and the vision of God will fall back again to the threshing floor and be gathered into the garner.

—The Church in the Time of Lawlessness

As the sword of truth exposes "the thoughts and attitudes of the heart," selfishness, hatred, hypocrisy, jealousy and pride often stand revealed where they have seethed beneath the surface affections of superficial human-centered love. Once pierced by truth, people must then choose whether to let that sword continue its work, until sin and its accompanying death are severed root and branch, or else they can lash out in resentment, clinging to pride, insisting that their false love is true, whereas God's true love is false. Finally, in their inner rage at the impotence of their own godhood, they often turn against the God of love who would deliver them, nailing Him in their hearts and minds once again to the cross of shame and so finally allowing the sharp edge of truth to cut them off from God instead of from sin. This can happen even with those who claim to follow this God, those who say, "Lord, Lord," but do not *do* His will.

—Leaving the Lonely Labyrinth

Matt. 7:21

Asleep to the Transcendent

So long as a person is centered in himself, his heart is hardened to one degree or another. But when we turn out from ourselves and toward God, and when His nature is engrafted within us, His heart and mind will come to be expressed through us.

—Building Christian Character

Some of the saddest and most tragic failures of human life come from people whose minds have fallen asleep to anything transcendent to themselves. Such minds look at the world in a way that reduces everyone else to the lowest common denominator of the immanent, the material, the natural—their only curiosity is about how everything and everyone might turn to "my good," "my pleasure," "my profit." This attitude secularizes the sacred. It causes people to see others merely in a public and desacralized way, merely in the way that they imagine that everyone else who matters sees them.

—Committed to Love

Character Dismantled Board by Board

Failure to confess sin incapacitates us for virtuous action: covering sin thwarts the ability to do God's will. Pilate knew that Jesus was innocent and should therefore be released; he even wanted to set Him free. But when he insisted that Jesus be set free, the ultra-Orthodox rabbinical Jews kept shouting, "If you let this man go, you are no friend of Caesar." Scripture says that, following this cry, Pilate brought Jesus out to the crowd and shortly afterward handed Him over to be crucified. Why would a Roman governor be intimidated by an alien mob's suggestion that he was "no friend of Caesar"? Historians describe Pilate's whole administration as rife with corruption and that the one thing he feared was an inspection by the Roman emperor.[7] To accuse him of being "no friend of Caesar" was to implicitly threaten such an investigation. The crowd well knew about his corrupt and weak character—that he had lied to and cheated those over him and then hidden it from them. Because of his past sins and the corruption of his administration—sins and corruption that he had sought to hide and cover up—he couldn't help Jesus, even though he seemed to want to, knowing as he did that the Nazarene was guiltless.

Because Pilate had, time after time, year after year, sought to hide his sin, when the ultimate test came, he could take no stand for truth and instead dipped his hand, in the very act of trying to wash it, into the blood of the crucified Lord. He had lived his life in the darkness of his lies. Board by board, with each lie, with each coverup, he had dismantled the house of any good character he might have

---

John 19:12; Luke 23:16

once possessed and thrown each board into a fire that gave only a temporary warmth to his naked exposure. This is all that his lies afforded him, until at last no substance was left of his life; and so at the great test, the moment of ultimate decision and destiny in his life, he crumbled to the pressure of the mob and aided and abetted the crucifixion of the Savior of the world. It is said that, like Judas, Pilate died at his own hand.

—*Building Christian Character*

The Call to Perfection

Be ye therefore perfect, even as your heavenly Father is perfect.

—*Matthew 5:48*

God's Spirit empowers us to ever strive to conform to the ultimate image of perfection. And God's Word defines that image. God calls us to perfection, and He will remain steadfast, unswerving from His purpose until it is accomplished. So, too, your goal must be total victory, a life and character fully integrated in oneness with God, completely reflecting His image. We cannot rest until not only our children but also we conform to the positive characteristics revealed in Scripture and are thus freed from all the negative characteristics that destroy human lives.

Yet in our press toward total victory, we should rejoice in and give thanks for every small step forward along the way. Remember, every victory is a supernatural gift of grace and must be received and appreciated as such. Remember also that mercy triumphs over judgment and that the Lord's long-suffering is our salvation. So while not compromising in any way the standards of God's Word, we always strive to see mercy triumph over justice.

—*Building Christian Character*

Rom. 8:29; Isa. 62:1-7; James 2:13; 2 Pet. 3:15

Part IV
"Teach Them to Your Children"

Aiming the Arrow

The goal of Christian education, like any goal or destination, at least in large part determines the principles and means by which we get there. In ancient Hebrew, the same word, *yarah*, means both "to shoot," as to shoot an arrow, and "to teach." *Yarah* is also the root of the word *moreh*, "teacher," as well as *torah*, which means literally "direction, instruction, law."

To "instruct" or "teach" is to aim for a goal, then to move in a foreordained direction toward that established destiny or goal. It is to send an arrow in flight from a bow toward a target. For Christians, the very image of God determines both our goal and our means for getting there. Since "God is one" and "God is love," the oneness (or wholeness) of love becomes our goal. This is true whether with God, within ourselves, with our fellow man or with creation. So the end does not justify merely any means we may choose but rather necessitates a means perfectly harmonious with the end.

—*Wisdom's Children*, Book Two

Educating the Whole Person

To fulfill our educational responsibilities, we must have this vision of the wholeness that God desires to bring forth in our children's lives. We must train them to be men and women of integrity, scrupulous and honest before God, undivided in their devotion to God.

All efforts in Christian education aim toward the whole person, a person brought into perfect relationship with his God, his fellow human beings and all of creation. Christian education trains the whole person to become fully at one in spirit, soul and body—living, acting, speaking and thinking in harmony, first, with God, fulfilling one's place in the kingdom from above. Moreover, the *tamim* (integrated or whole) individual takes dominion only *under God* and in order to expand God's own dominion of love into every area given to the positive influence of that individual. To learn to exercise any dominion under God necessarily means to see ourselves as always unfolding on some level into God's image, but this exercise of the rule of love touches *every* area of existence.

—*Wisdom's Children, Books One and Two*

---

1 Thess. 5:23

Parental Relationship

Train up a child in the way he should go, and when he is old he will not depart from it.

—*Proverbs 22:6*

Children are born into families, born into a natural relationship with their parents. So from the very beginning of history, parents have always functioned as the natural educators of their children, and such an educational process unfolds through a *specific form* of relationship. Parents encourage and help the child to walk, to talk, to play, to sing, to do all that growing and maturing entails, through *relationship*.

The child learns perhaps more of the essentials of life *primarily* through relationship with his parents (and maybe also with older, responsible brothers or sisters) than in any other way. The parental relationship, in other words, provides the natural context for all unfolding impartation of a given relational knowledge in all of its ramifications, settings and levels. This is the knowledge that can alone help the child unfold into the full integrity and wholeness of mature character.

—*Wisdom's Children, Book One*

Simply the amount of affection, of love that's shown toward a baby that can't talk or do anything to respond, does something even to the very neural structure of the brain of this infant put into our hands for relationship. What that child is going to become will depend on the nature of the attachments that are made from the earliest moments of life.

—*So-o-o Emotional*

The birth and rearing of a child is a rite of passage for *all those* committed to life, no matter what the cost, because they value life itself above merely preserving their own existence or comforts. In birth and education, then, we go far, often without even knowing it, in determining which of two powers will bind us together as a family: the love of life or the fear of death, the internal power of God's love or the external forces of compulsion.

—*Wisdom's Children, Book One*

Parental Initiative

Children, obey your parents in the Lord, for this is right. "Honor your father and mother," which is the first commandment with promise: "that it may be well with you and you may live long on the earth." And you, fathers, do not provoke your children to wrath, but bring them up in the training and admonition of the Lord.

—Ephesians 6:1-4

As parents we must overcome the inertia—the death—that would cause us to idly sit waiting for someone else to take initiative in our children's lives. It's up to us to take the initiative and press forward into life. We must stand convicted before God that He holds us liable for the training of our children and that we as parents possess the God-given love to accomplish this task. Nothing else will give rise to the abiding initiative required to accomplish the training and discipleship necessary to raise sons and daughters of God.

As we fully accept our liability and responsibility before God for the rearing of our children, we choose life over death. This initiative may show us our own need to find our own place in the supportive relationships of God's larger family—a local expression of the Body that sees the importance of such a vision; but each day, if we will make the sacrifices to walk in obedience to His revealed will, God will empower us to overcome the obstacles to life that would prevent us from accomplishing His great purpose.

As we overcome these obstacles, we can hope to see our children grow to become the children of wisdom—the children of that cohesive power which is life. And as God imparts through us the overcoming power of life unto our children, that power grows also within us as we make our own home in His Word and become His disciples indeed. Then both parents and their offspring can hope to become God's children, Wisdom's children.

—*Wisdom's Children, Book One*

John 8:31-32

The Strength of Conviction

The narrowing of legal strictures has underscored that even beyond the arena of legal defense, Christian home schoolers now discern a greater need for a different strength, the strength of conviction, in order to *spiritually* stand against both the brute force of State power and the spiritual seduction of an increasingly desacralized culture with its free-writhing way of life and its lukewarm church.

The last threadbare remnants of constitutionally guaranteed religious freedoms in this country depend not only upon whether beliefs find their "source" in religion, but also whether Christian lives express the depth, consistency and sincerity of those beliefs.

—Education Exodus

Opposite Views, Opposite Gods

Therefore you shall lay up these words of mine in your heart and in your soul, and bind them as a sign on your hand, and they shall be as frontlets between your eyes. You shall teach them to your children, speaking of them when you sit in your house, when you walk by the way, when you lie down, and when you rise up.

—*Deuteronomy 11:18-19*

The Judeo-Christian view for millennia contended that education was a means to disciple the child in faith and submission to the Spirit and Word of a transcendent deity. The human-centered view, the view of a now thoroughly desacralized humanism, contended that the function of education was to teach the child that he himself is the only god he'll ever know or need to know.

The inescapably religious character of education was, for Christians, underscored by the fact that the history of education is, fundamentally, the history of conflict between basically antagonistic religious worldviews. Dr. Frederick Mayer, speaking from the secular perspective, contended that "throughout the history of education two philosophies have fought for dominance."[8] While some took issue with the precise way in which he drew the lines between these two philosophies, in general his fundamental distinction was between those who portray man as an imperfect, lapsed being redeemable only by the grace of a transcendent God (the Judeo-Christian view) and those who believe that man is essentially his own god, so that, in Mayer's words, "the function of education is to point out what the greatest pleasures are."[9]

—*Education Exodus*

Education: The Conflict for Control

The history of education can be viewed as a conflict between the Judeo-Christian belief in a transcendent God, on the one hand, and the various modes of belief in an immanent human godhood, on the other. These beliefs in human godhood have, to use Johns Hopkins professor Kingsley Price's terms, sought to "eliminate" any transcendent God from education, desacralizing all public schooling by putting man and "World-Spirit" in such a God's place.

The State's principal concern in overseeing the schooling of children had never been the educational development of its charges but merely maintaining its own control over the educational process.

The incontestable point, from every perspective, was that every legal system must be interwoven with a *system of values*. This, of course, would include a system that was jailing parents, chaining church doors, seizing some children and forcing others into public schools.

The very issue in the conflict of control of children could not, then, be separated from the more basic conflict that had raised this question in the first place: the conflict between, on the one hand, a religion of an anthropocentric relativism, ultimately expressed in the absolute power of a compulsory, humanistic State, and, on the other hand, a transcendent absolute ultimately expressed in a non-coercive and voluntary religion such as that of certain strands of the Judeo-Christian tradition going back to its beginnings.

Now, however, because they finally recognized that all values and laws do, in fact, rest on some religion, believers have begun to experience an often surging desire to rediscover just what their own values and culture would look like if these consistently rested on their professed religion, thus providing an entire counterproposal to the surrounding culture.

—*Education Exodus*

Which Kingdom and Culture?

Failure to train children in the way they should go, to inform their minds with and conform their lives to a living, relational knowledge of God, will without doubt deliver them into the maw of their soul's greatest enemy.

—Wisdom's Children, Book One

Do we seek to find the context of our child's life in a desacralized world or in an alternative culture called "the kingdom of God," the Body of Christ? Do we even see the Body of Christ as the alternative culture the courts apparently view it as, one in the context of which our children even *could* possibly find their places within a consistent, Christocentric way of life, or does our Christianity merely encompass meetings, seminars, other parachurch activities and socials, with the church serving as a spiritually validating adjunct, a sort of chaplaincy function, to the kingdoms of the world? Are Christian lives "complete in Him," as Paul said believers' lives in Christ should be, or do we live most of our lives not only "in the world" but in a way that inevitably makes us seem inextricably "of the world"? Where is the kingdom of God "not of this world"?

—*Education Exodus*

Which Kind of Knowledge?

Only within our limits can we come into proper relationship with—and therefore relational knowledge of—the portion of creation that God places within our finite hands.

The root of the knowledge of life, unlike the fallen knowledge of "good and evil," does not lie in the reasonings of the human-centered mind, subject as that latter mind is to a cosmic disintegration, corruption and decay, but in the transcendent, unchanging, eternal Spirit of the One who has created all things, including the finite mind.

These two different kinds of knowledge—one inducing the Fall and the other bringing salvation—correspond, then, to two different perspectives: the anthropocentric or pagan perspective as opposed to the theocentric, Judeo-Messianic perspective. Only the God-centered perspective can bring the wholeness or coherence that Christian education strives for, since only a singular God of such impartial vision that He could be said, in one sense, to be situated equidistantly from (or at one with) all things can serve as the cohesive Center who can bring all things into coherence around Himself. Jesus defined eternal life as "*knowing* . . . the only true God and Jesus Christ" whom God had sent (John 17:3).

So we become centered in the One God of Israel by becoming centered in the knowledge of God deposited in Jesus. The knowledge of God made manifest and personified in Jesus then becomes both the end and the means of all true Christian education.

—Wisdom's Children, Book One

---

1 Cor. 2:11-12

Teaching Children to Seek God

They received the word with all readiness, and searched the Scriptures daily to find out whether these things were so.

—Acts 17:11

We see the goal of our Christian educational process as a fruitful, mature, responsible, loving individual, someone able to follow the Spirit of God and to be directed by the Word of God, a person who has real, living relationships with God, with God's people and with God's creation. Such a person has begun to perceive and understand the relationships between things—and thus their meaning—in a way that enables him to act in the Spirit to accomplish God's purpose.

Just as our first goal must be to rear children who primarily depend on the Spirit and Word of God rather than on other people, so the basic purpose of Christian education must be "to teach men how to learn for themselves," that is, how to be taught directly by the Spirit.[10] The book of Acts tells us that the students of Berea were counted as more "noble" because they investigated the truth of Paul's teachings for themselves by searching the Scriptures, and so were able to confirm directly from the Scriptures the words he spoke. We want our children to learn to do this on every level: to learn how to hear and be taught by the Great Teacher, not merely for the sake of learning as some abstract and arrogant end in itself, but in order that they may, through a transcendently rooted wisdom, establish God's dominion over the earth.

We must teach them the principles that will enable them to seek God and overcome all of the individual pockets of ignorance that stand in the way of establishing God's dominion, whether in their life or in all they are responsible for. We can, in short, lead them onto the path that will take them, in every situation and circumstance, to God's knowledge of the whole. Because they always know how to find God's vision through prayer that brings them into God's Spirit, they will always be able to fulfill completely their God-given responsibilities.

—*Wisdom's Children, Book Two*

Going to the Source

True education must aim to bring us to that place of spiritual and intellectual maturity where we can receive everything we need from God to accomplish this purpose (whether through our brothers and sisters, through books and other research or directly from the Spirit). We must learn how to work with others and how to submit, but we must also learn to personally acquire the information and the skills we need to bring forth that part of God's vision that He would entrust into our hands. This includes His vision for marriage, children and families.

We must see everything that our children learn as pointing beyond the subject or the facts at hand and back to the Source of all true knowledge and wisdom. Everything they learn must gently direct them to that personal relationship with the Spirit of God who will faithfully lead and guide them into all truth.

—*Wisdom's Children, Book Two*

Overcoming That We Might Give

Many feel a lack within themselves—that, for example, they have a desire to give their children a deeper understanding of history but feel too ignorant to do so. One of the advantages about home education, however, is that it forces us as parents to overcome our own ignorance. Perhaps we can make excuses for ourselves and try to just get by, but if we want more than that for our children, then we must have more than that ourselves. Our children can't come into the fullness of their inheritance unless we come into the fullness of ours, because an inheritance is handed down from parent to child, and the parents can only give what they themselves possess.

Just as we can't have successful Christian schooling unless the child is properly connected to his parents, so we can't have successful home education unless the parent is properly connected to those ministries through which the Head ministers His truth into the parents' lives.

If you first gain a conviction that God has given you the responsibility and the capacity to train your child, that He has placed you in a unique and ideal relationship with your child to meet all his real needs and to do so much more effectively than can anyone else, and if you don't lose your grip of faith on this conviction, then God will make a way for you to accomplish what needs to be done.

—Wisdom's Children, Book One

John 3:27

Inheritance of the Anointed Word

We must train up a generation that will not merely repeat what their parents have said but, while clinging to every godly pattern and truth they have inherited from their parents, will also be able to speak the *current* Word, the *rhema* that God has ordained for their own time, a Word founded solidly in the unchanging Word of the eternal *logos*.

To fail to engage in such a dialectic with the world for our own day will either leave us isolated by our failure to relate the truths of God to the current situation in the world or else will find us captivated by the world. We will become captives of the world because we will fail to see that all that unfolds in it has meaning only as an opportunity for the church to address itself to the honest hearted and to present the needed alternative. For those who fail to see this, the world will become their only alternative, and they will literally lose themselves in it and its political and economic systems of power and greed.

Unless we train our children so that they may find the fullness of God for their own lives for their own day and thus fulfill their function for their day, we, too, stand in danger of condemning them to either irrelevance or co-optation. We—and then our children—must penetrate through to see how exactly the trends of the times are preparing human hearts to receive the light of Christ, and then we must express that light in terms relevant to these times. Otherwise, we will either end up sterile in our isolation or deceived into going along with the trends of the world.

—*Wisdom's Children, Book Two*

The Maturity of Wisdom

We must raise up children to express God's attributes in their whole lives, as part of a whole people who live in continual and harmonious relationship with the living God, and so live in harmony in His patterns of relationship with their fellow man and with creation as well.

The whole of our lives unfolds as a struggle to attain to the wisdom, the maturity, of Christ. The first stage can be seen as the grammar level, the period of childhood and adolescence, where most of life consists of acquiring knowledge, learning the elementary lessons of living.

The next stage, from adolescence to perhaps approximately the age of fifty or even later, becomes the dialectic stage. In this stage, everything centers on the conflict to bring to resolution doubtful propositions. Life is a battle and a testing to come to stability on every level until at last one can stand secure, spiritually and in other respects as well. Finally, one can then move into the realm of rhetoric, of wisdom.

But one cannot come to this wisdom of the "mature" without passing through, as we've said, the stages of spiritual growth that lead to this maturity. God does not anoint an empty head, but as we exert effort to learn the elementary principles of the grammar stage and the systems of truth of the dialectic stage, then God's Spirit can take that truth and anoint it for a proclamation in love. This constitutes the level of wisdom: when truth is ministered by the Spirit, when God's people have come to maturity as a perfect man who, not singly, but together as a corporate whole, constitutes the total proclamation of the love and truth of Jesus Christ, not only in word but also and especially in deed as well. Then, in our whole lives and beings, we will become His image on the earth.

—Wisdom's Children, Book Two

Wisdom Builds Her House

So we can define the goal of Christian education as the nurturing of a whole person, a person who lives in ever-perfecting and more harmonious relationship with God, with his fellow man and with creation. The goals of wholeness and wisdom do not really differ, however, for only wisdom can bring forth a life of wholeness, and such a life can only then be lived out through wisdom.

But what is wisdom? How exactly can one define its nature and describe its workings? Wisdom is the ability to perceive relationships, not only particular, individual relationships, but the whole interlinked series and patterns of relationships within which any individual person, thing or act can truly live. This self-evidently requires a view of reality transcendent to merely human viewpoints. Wisdom enables us to perceive the form, the pattern of relationships, in which any individual act takes place, to recognize the fullness of all the interrelationships between that individual act and the wide diversity of its effects and ramifications. Wisdom, then, gives us the ability to bring something forth in wholeness, completeness, the ability to see the proper form in which something must exist in order to develop into the fullness that God intended.

Wisdom builds her house. Wisdom perceives the living form into which everything must fit together, the form of life that gives meaning to it all: the form of the Body of Christ, the animate patterns for a viable agrarian community that maintains and passes on both natural and spiritual life, the perfect form to hold the fullest content of an individual's life, the living patterns for a family sustaining the continuity of life, so that each and all might be properly framed together in the perfect will and life of the eternal God. Wisdom brings forth a truly whole person, and through wisdom such a person lives a life in which every component part and act has the fullness of meaning, purpose and benefit that God has arranged for it. It is therefore wisdom that we must seek, both for ourselves and for our children and our children's children.

—*Wisdom's Children, Book Two*

James 1:5; Prov. 4:7

Part V
Work as Worship

What Is Craft?

Craftsmanship reveals the significance of the spiritual in material terms.

—*Craft: The Art of Work*

A craft is any work discipline that holds in check any noise of human flesh and frees the soul to sing for a moment.

If the making of a thing is a craft, and craft is a response to the highest of motives, then no one can ultimately give someone else the machinelike specifications of how the craft is to be made. Directions and instructions on techniques and principles can and must be given. But the making of the thing is a form of worship, and no one can worship for you.

The task of the craftsman, it has been said, is to "make well what needs making—for the love of God and for the service of our fellow men and women."

—*Craft: The Art of Work*

Manual Is Not Menial

By the sweat of your brow you will eat your food until you return to the ground, since from it you were taken; for dust you are and to dust you will return.

—*Genesis 3:19*

When man and woman first came down from the tree—the tree of knowledge—they came down not with a club but with a hoe in hand and an idea in mind. A post-lapsarian world made work necessary for life; but precisely because it was necessary and sustained life, it could not be all bad. If this was so, then no essential or necessary work could in itself be considered demeaning.

Yet today's world has been possessed of the notion that manual work is somehow intrinsically degrading and must by any means be escaped. The industrialized world filled its factories by encouraging this notion that all and any physical labor involving essentials—growing food or making one's shelter, furnishings and clothing—was "drudgery" and fit only for "drones."

Manual labor is, in short, simply essential for life and, when directed to responsibly producing what is essential for life, can be both holy and honorable. So drudgery does not inhere in the nature of physical work itself but in certain degraded conditions that must follow from the assumptions and practices of urbanism, industrialism and mass-market commercialism.

Of course, we today look back at the work of the millions pulled off their family farms and into what soon became urban industrial ghettos, toiling like slaves in factories, sweatshops, mines, transport warehouses and docks, or on monocrop agribusiness factory farms, and all such labor now seems obviously a degrading drudgery that ought to have been replaced by machinery if for nothing else than to relieve physical and mental distress. Yet what defined the drudgery in all this was not manual work itself, but the factorial and mechanically repetitious nature of a work that lies outside the rhythm of times and seasons and that negated the knowing, willing, loving human response to higher relationships not only with nature but also both with the divine and with the human community.

—*Craft: The Art of Work*

Labor Is Worship

Love the Lord your God with all your heart and with all your soul and with all your mind and with all your strength.

—*Mark 12:30*

The notion of work only for profit arose out of the desacralization, the secularization, of life, which removed the significance of all spiritual considerations and relationships from daily human work and thus made such work utterly profane, material, menial and so a "drudgery" indeed. As a result of such profanation of work, only concerns for material comfort and convenience were now offered as the standard by which to measure the worth of an activity. This was in turn rooted in the attitude historically associated with that of the slave, who also worked only for his physical well-being—to be fed, avoid punishment and such.

On the other hand, some have seen in this profanation of work a type of professionalism that finds its archetype in the "work" of the courtesan, who views her body as a means of profit rather than as merely one avenue of a covenant relationship meant to touch and embrace *all* life. The slave or prostitute has no sense of responsibility beyond physical survival, pleasure, profit, convenience or comfort. The free man works for something higher: *Laborare est orare*—"Labor is worship." His work is sacred, holy, and therefore overflows with meaning.

—*Craft: The Art of Work*

The Sacredness of Work

If all of life is viewed as falling within the realm of the sacred, then all of life becomes exceedingly meaningful. What one does in order to live is always more meaningful than play. This is necessarily so because work can be consecrated to serving the higher purpose of sustaining life, while leisure seldom if ever is. Therefore, the latter becomes quickly meaningless and boring. (Of course, even recreation can be consecrated to serve the larger purpose of vocation when it is truly to re-create, renew, us to serve our larger calling in life.) When such a meaning permeates life, then work becomes enjoyable because what fulfills—what fills us full of meaning—is what truly causes us to rejoice.

Work, then, only becomes a "drudgery" to be escaped in empty play when it is mechanically repetitive and cut off from its direct participation in sustaining life, leaving only the meaning of money or "success" or "status." When work is deeply involved in and related to the essentials of life—raising food to eat, giving birth to life, nurturing that life and then dying with dignity and in love at the end of a full life—there is no "drudgery," for meaning and fulfillment displace drudgery. Such work is sacred because the life it sustains is sacred.

When labor loses this sense of the sacred, leisure lapses into idolatry—and people lose any higher aspirations than merely "having fun." They become devotees of a fanaticism whose only dogma is "feel good." Interestingly enough, the words *fun* and *fool* share the same root: it is easy to be "tricked" or "fooled" by the "funny" or the "fun."

—*Craft: The Art of Work*

A Response to the Highest Calling

> *Some have distinguished craft from at least one sort of labor: craft elevates matter to something that expresses the reconciliation of creator and created; debased labor creates machines that express only power.*
>
> —*Craft: The Art of Work*

The essential beauty and perfection of, say, the work put into a handmade chair comes from the craftsman's response to the highest calling, to the love of God, to which the chair then bears witness. It is not so, however, with factory-made things: no one can be held responsible before God for a factory-made chair, because no single individual was responsible for making it. Therefore it was not made as a response to love but, as the slave or prostitute works, as a response to doing what one is told to do, perhaps simply for money and for little or nothing else. Someone else, in short, must always stand ultimately responsible for the slave's work.

Any system that in this way nullifies human responsibility in the doing of quality work can even be seen as essentially un-Christian because it negates that part of human beings that distinguishes them from beasts. Mass machine manufacturing reduces our humanity, our souls. It uses us to mass-produce items less and less reflective of any higher human aspirations. These items do not reflect the intent of knowing, willing, loving people made in God's image. In order to meet the demand for cheaper quantities in greater numbers, manufactured objects become increasingly unsuitable for truly human life and even cheapen the quality of that life. Instead they often seem fit only for creatures (such as a donkey) that merely use, transform and recycle nature but that, unlike people, have never been known to consciously create anything that never existed before. Animals may communicate on some level, but they do not generally cook meals and sit at tables they have made for aesthetic appeal to eat those meals in the enjoyment of fellowship with other like beings.

—*Craft: The Art of Work*

Recapturing the Meaning of Work

Our own homestead community's desire to recapture the meaning of work by preserving those crafts so tied to the essentials of human existence is not a desire for a nostalgic return to some quaint picture of the past in the hopes of finding perfect and unalloyed happiness in this world. The past offered only steppingstones, but our age has thrown away many of the necessary stones that once seemed to carry humankind toward a more desirable reality and destiny. It is this reality that the best of the distilled past pointed to, but had not yet fulfilled, and that we still seek. So we also first seek to restore any fit and well-placed stones given us by the past. Only then can we finish laying new stones that will take us further down the same path walked by those of our working forefathers and mothers who better knew the enlightened way.

Any joy that material things bring us becomes truly justifiable insofar as these things become a foretaste and symbol of a more enduring joy, a sign and promise of a greater destination in an everlasting kingdom where love never ends. For those who hold such a view, the world is less titillating and dazzling. So the true artist does not seek prizes, awards, titles, offices, flattery, prestige, pampering and spoiling or any honored place. He seeks only honorable work. The true artist, whose very life is art, is abnormally normal, a simple maker and doer of things.

—*Craft: The Art of Work*

Art Expresses Religion

Let your light so shine before men, that they may see your good works and glorify your Father in heaven.

—Matthew 5:16

As we find the reality we seek, we then want to not merely talk about but portray that reality by living it; and that portrayal will be of a workaday existence lived in the purpose and presence of the sacred, and therefore a life full of meaning. The material results of such a life will be in creatures well trained and things well made—draft horses or oxen (and sheep dogs, too), as well as food crops, furniture, pottery, fabrics, metal work—useful things for people whose vision is directed heavenward. In this simplicity of vision, we hope to escape the snare of turning mere art by itself into our religion; we hope instead to make art express our religion. This will transform the idol into a craft and the stereotypically flattered and vain artist into the honest workman who serves his fellow man in love. This is true whether the art is pots or songs or beautifully lived lives.

—*Craft: The Art of Work*

"Why Do You Do It?"

Love, which alone truly profits (as Paul tells us in the thirteenth chapter of First Corinthians), is the sum of all meaning. And to us, meaning and fulfillment supply much better criteria than does money when it comes to establishing the worth of one's "time and effort." What is "worth my time" is what is meaningful to me, to my people and to my God. If it "means" something in this context, then it is worth my "time and effort." Relationship supplies such a meaning, and homesteading skills and crafts take place in a plexus of relationships with creation, creatures and Creator that make them exceedingly meaningful—so meaningful, in fact, that they are sacred—and, therefore, always worthwhile. Our community life, we hope, can also prove worthwhile by conveying to you, the reader, a glimpse into, a remembrance of, the purpose of the vanishing art of a work that is life. Hopefully, it will then provide some answer to those who ask, "Why do you do it?"

—*Craft: The Art of Work*

Beauty: The Outshining of Order

But everything should be done in a fitting and orderly way.

—1 Corinthians 14:40

When something is well made, we say it is beautiful. What, however, constitutes its beauty? A critical constituent of beauty would seem to be a due *order*. The word *order*, which shares roots with the word *art*, relates all the parts into an expressively proportionate whole in the givens of life. Beauty is the conspicuous outshining of an order that puts the mind of him who beholds it at rest, at peace, in the sense that the mind feels fulfilled and finds joy in the fullness. This also defines the visible expression of what is holy. This outshining enlightens in some way the soul of the beholder. The object becomes not something known in itself but an avenue of knowledge, a source of revelation. It draws us, somehow inarticulately, to truth.

—*Craft: The Art of Work*

Work That Speaks

The art of work is the work of art.
—*Craft: The Art of Work*

A craft, as distinct from a manufacture, is an *expression* of something within the person. As such, it has the potential to speak to others—that is, to bear witness to life in a way more than merely verbal. A whole lifestyle can become a message of exceedingly good news.

There is no need for the craftsman to endlessly talk about beauty, truth and so on, or even to be able to do so. The craftsman works most wisely who is not conscious of his own wisdom but only of its highest Source.

The good craftsman works with no thought that he is an artist. Such self-consciousness hinders the motive power that transcends human beings and that is their first and final cause for working. "Self-forgetfulness, self-abnegation, is the proper state of mind for man. Thus, and thus alone, can he collaborate with God." Only then can he be conscious of God and can say, "The dayspring from on high has visited us," and so in his craft "carry on that visitation."

—*Craft: The Art of Work*

Art as Virtue

Art is only a virtue when it makes and does well what is needed, whether fitting drainpipes, gardening, cooking, teaching, composing, singing, practicing at bar, homemaking, painting, furniture making, pottery making, spinning, weaving, writing or farming. Such an art is a service always rooted in the sacred. It becomes a handmaiden to God. Technique, or technology and the science that feeds it, can only find its legitimacy and proper place when it is reduced from its godlike status and becomes subservient as the handmaiden of such art.

When you say: "I don't know what's good or bad art—I only know what I like," this is a perfectly legitimate saying: you like what pleases you, as well you should. We only ask, as we do of our craftsmen, that you take the time and effort necessary to exercise your soul, heart and mind—your equipment for liking—and so keep them fit to like what is good.

—Craft: The Art of Work

The Craftsman as a Conduit

The craftsman is he who receives and passes on a creative power greater than himself. Craft moves through a plexus of relationships that reconcile the "above" (the Master, or the creative power of God) with the "below" (the apprentice, or craftsman himself). As such, it bears witness to the human purpose on earth and so of human nature itself. This individual who stands in his place is the traditional bridge between the transcendent and the immanent, between heaven and earth: the *imago dei* (image of God). Craft also can become one means by which a person may build a bridge between his soul and his livelihood and thereby center his work and daily life in God's transcendent unity. From the interaction of the movement from above (the creative source) to below (the workman and his work) and back again comes the transformation of the craftsman: the one in whom the movements meet. So we hold to the traditional view of craft as one means to bear witness to a potential human oneness with God and therefore to the potential wholeness that can come as a result.

—*Craft: The Art of Work*

To Express the Love of God

Every craftsman knows that his raw material has a character and potential unlike any other. He must learn this character by touch, sight, hearing and understanding. Then a relationship appears between it and his own character. He accepts a pattern for his craft that is not "his" but one given to him from above. Yet his work is not merely to obey and copy, nor to "expedite natural processes," but to bring forth something uniquely his, some part of himself, and to unite this part of himself with the material in his hands so that he might participate in the reconciliation of all things and elevate even inert matter to express the love of God. Otherwise, no relationship comes, the material remains inert, and he continues himself being nothing more than an industrialized laborer.

—Craft: The Art of Work

Responsibility Makes a Craftsman

If you bear full responsibility for what you do, then you have the potential to be a craftsman, and what you use in the doing is a tool. As your responsibility is diminished by the automatic nature in the process of what is being made, then your identity as a craftsman is also being diminished; and you are on your way to becoming simply another component in "unit production costs." With a tool, the craftsman has greater control. A tool, unlike a machine, is never the primary focus of attention. Its use becomes subsidiary, and all attention is released to focus on the work itself.

—*Craft: The Art of Work*

Serving Creation

The work of the shepherd in lambing season, the work of the farmer in spring plowing, of the stoneworker, the potter, the cabinetmaker, the spinner, the weaver, the homemaker, the husbandman, the metalsmith—all are venerable because they hang on the personal knowledge, will and love of the craftsman, who has assumed responsibility for the results and quality of what his or her words and work effect. Such craftsmen are individual human beings, persons who serve creation, their fellow men and God.

—*Craft: The Art of Work*

A Calling

Every individual is called to God's love and to share that love through the work of his hands. So every individual is called to be an artist, at least in the original sense of that word: the God-given power in every person to so direct the will and actions that the result of his thoughts and deeds is a responsible thing made that expresses a beauty beyond its original raw material.

It is futile to complain about the world and our lives, claiming to want better, if we remain unwilling to examine the foundations of our lives and their meaning. One place to begin examining foundations is in that part of life that consumes the largest portion of human existence: our work, our vocations. A vocation means literally a "calling," but a calling necessitates a Caller. So a vocation is a call first to share in God's own life, which places our ultimate destinations beyond the natural world and makes our natural lives and callings here a means to educate us to our ultimate calling.

—*Craft: The Art of Work*

"For the Joy Set before Us"

If we physically strain to overcome a recalcitrant stone in the path of our plowshare, and in so doing feel the pangs in our muscles as they try to grow stronger and overcome the passivity of the uncreative life, do we not often secretly rejoice in our small "sufferings"? If, however, we reach for an object and pain shoots through our back, we know something is wrong. If we eat something and a noxious taste fills our mouth rather than pleasure, we know something is wrong. So, too, when we work and find no fulfillment in it, something is wrong. Even pain knows joy when it accompanies good labor, as in the birth of a child or when individuals pour themselves out for causes greater than themselves. Or when a Savior suffers death on a cross.

—*Craft: The Art of Work*

Part VI
The "Full Declaration"

Knowing the Only True God

You worship what you do not know; we know what we worship, for salvation is of the Jews.

—John 4:22

And this is eternal life, that they may know You, the only true God, and Jesus Christ whom You have sent.

—John 17:3

Jesus, according to His own words in John 4:22, did not claim to bring a revelation of the nature of God that differed from that of Moses and the prophets. On the contrary, He confirmed the original Judaic revelation—"Salvation is of the Jews," and that salvation has to do with "knowing what we worship." It is not surprising, then, that when asked which was the first and greatest commandment, Jesus replied, "The most important one is this: 'Hear, O Israel, the Lord our God, the Lord is one. Love the Lord your God with all your heart and with all your soul and with all your mind and with all your strength'" (Mark 12:29-30).

Furthermore, when asked for the central tenet of His faith, Jesus pointed back to this same Judaic revelation of the nature of "the only true God," the God of Israel, the Father (John 17:3). So in that passage in John 17:3, Jesus declared to the Father: "This is *eternal life*: that they may *know You*, the *only true God*, and Jesus Christ, whom You have sent." Since eternal life is salvation, God's very purpose in bringing human lives into oneness with Himself rests upon their clear knowledge of this revelation, this knowledge, of "the only true God."

Luke 19:10; Eph. 3:10-11

To distort God's nature and its incarnation in Christ is to destroy the chance of human salvation, of authentically knowing the only true God. Thus, also, Jesus' troubling words: "If you believe not that I am He, you shall die in your sins" (John 8:24). Why? Because it means you have not truly come to know "the only true God."

—*The Messianic Incarnation*

The Central Revelation of the New Testament

And the Word became flesh and dwelt among us, and we beheld His glory, the glory as of the only begotten of the Father, full of grace and truth.

—John 1:14

The incarnation provides the central revelation of the New Testament. In it, the piecemeal glimpses of God's nature presented throughout the Old Testament era—whether directly through prophecy or symbolically through the tabernacle, the temple, the festivals, the ceremonial law and so on—now, in the New Testament, focus and articulate themselves into an integrated life and speak through the same flesh and blood that all humanity in all its sufferings and needs moves in.

—*The Messianic Incarnation*

Complete Unity

In the beginning was the Word, and the Word was with God, and the Word was God. He was in the beginning with God. All things were made through Him, and without Him nothing was made that was made. In Him was life, and the life was the light of men. And the light shines in the darkness, and the darkness did not comprehend it.

—John 1:1-5

For in Him dwells all the fullness of the Godhead bodily; and you are complete in Him.

—Colossians 2:9-10

And the glory which You gave Me I have given them, that they may be one just as We are one: I in them, and You in Me; that they may be made perfect in one, and that the world may know that You have sent Me, and have loved them as You have loved Me.

—John 17:22-23

This full scope of oneness, of fellowship—with the Father, with the Son, with our fellow man and with creation—becomes possible because "the fullness of God" has now "dwelt in *bodily* form" (Col. 2:9)—that is, within the constraints of the very form that we ourselves (as lapsed and death-bound human beings) live in, the Great God has appeared, as if the King had left His palace to wear our rags and come among us in our suffering. The Creator of *all* creation has *fully* manifested Himself *within* fallen creation; He has Himself demonstrated that humanity and deity can become one in the man Christ Jesus.

Moreover, the *full* revelation of God in "the *man* Christ

Jesus" tells us how complete the unity of His corporate Body can now be, just how deeply and totally we can share our lives within His covenant—Jesus spoke explicitly of this, and so did John. This revelation of *God* in "the *man* Christ Jesus" also provided the means for fallen humanity to find atonement—at-one-ment—for, through this innocent, sinless man's sacrificial love, a love unto death, humanity could be reconciled with God and overcome death.

—*The Messianic Incarnation*

John 17:21, 23; 1:1-8

The Full Declaration

He is the image of the invisible God, the firstborn over all creation . . . . And He is the head of the body, the church, who is the beginning, the firstborn from the dead, that in all things He may have the preeminence.

—Colossians 1:15-18

No one has seen God at any time. The only begotten Son, who is in the bosom of the Father, He has declared Him.

—John 1:18

Jesus came to bring the *full* declaration, the *full* manifestation, of the nature, Being and presence of the God of redeeming love directly into human lives. He came, in short, as the perfect and whole—the living—communication of God to humankind, the Word made flesh.

Jesus was *not* the incarnation of the "eternal Son"; He was the incarnation of the eternal Father!

—The Messianic Incarnation

John 1:1-3, 17-18; 10:30; 14:9

The Unfolding Revelation of God's Nature

This relationship of the eternal God to humankind began with the call of Abraham out of Ur. God was calling him to a new order of relationships, one that would ascend rather than descend. This relationship between the human and the divine then unfolded in the revelation of the One God, first, as the God of creation and of immutable law—*Elohim*; then, as the God of mercy in the revelation of *El Shaddai*; and finally as the Being One who continually reveals Himself in unfolding and ever more direct relationship—*Yahweh*. (The Hebrew root of the name Yahweh is the word for "being."[11])

So the revelation of Yahweh did not cease at its beginning with Moses. The "self-existent One who continually reveals Himself" (as the name *Yahweh* can be interpreted to mean) would continually unfold His nature to His people. The "I will become whatsoever I will become" would now become whatever His people needed in order to bring them into at-one-ment with Himself. He would become, in an unfolding revelation: first, Yahweh-Yireh, their provider; then, Yahweh-Nissi, their banner; next, Yahweh-Rophecha, their healer; and Yahweh-Mekaddishkem, their sanctifier; and Yahweh-Shalom, their peace; Yahweh-Rohi, their shepherd; Yahweh-Tsidkenu, their righteousness; and, becoming ever more immediate and closer, Yahweh-Shammah, Yahweh is present.

But, finally, in the fullest, most intimate, personal and complete revelation of Himself, He would become Yahweh-Hoshea, Yahweh their salvation. This would be

---

Exod. 6:2; 3:14; 17:15; 15:26; 31:13; Gen. 22:14; Judg. 6:24; Ps. 23:1; Jer. 23:5-6; Ezek. 48:35; Matt. 1:21

the consummation of all the unveilings of God, bringing humanity and deity increasingly together as one. This would be God and man united in one image, one person—Messiah. Thus the Hebrew name *Yahshua* comes from the contraction of Yahweh-Hoshea, meaning, "Yahweh saves." This is the meaning of the name *Jesus*, which in Hebrew is *Yahshua*.

—*The Messianic Incarnation*

God's Authority

In the Judaic view, only *God's* own authority is absolute and unconditional. He is the sole, supreme ruler, and the power He rules by is love. All other authority, at least in terms of our required obedience before God, remains relative and conditional to our required obedience to God's authority. These conditional authorities include: that of parents, of husbands and wives, of governments, of the church, of angels—all are subject to the limitations imposed upon them by the One universal Sovereign.

If we remove this clear understanding of the absolute authority of the One God, any absolute limit upon human authority automatically and alarmingly ceases. Hence, belief in the absolute oneness of God ultimately becomes the only effective check against an unlimited tyrannical authority, such as those of twentieth-century Statists and totalitarians. For this very reason the ontological trinitarian viewpoint was so adaptable to the purposes of State rulers in the later Roman Empire in what we see as the Constantinian synthesis and also to such later proponents of Statism as Hegel and Marx, whose trinitarian philosophical framework contributed greatly to confusing the human understanding of history and was the progenitor of two of the most formidable modern expressions of Statism (and also two of the most formidable persecutors of both Jews and Christians). I'm speaking of Fascism and Marxism, that is, National Socialism and International Socialism, Nazism and Internazism.[12]

He who is the Source of all authority, the Spirit, has *delegated all authority unto the Son. The Son is God manifested in the flesh. In the flesh itself,* the Son was a created Being through whom the almighty God fully manifested Himself.

—*The Messianic Incarnation*

---

1 Tim. 3:16

Jesus' Twofold Nature

In the flesh, Jesus was a man; in the Spirit, He was God. In the flesh, He was the Son; in the Spirit, He was the Father. In the flesh, He was tempted by satan; in the Spirit, He cast out satan. In the flesh, He ate; in the Spirit, He multiplied the bread and fish. In the flesh, as a man, He prayed at the grave of Lazarus; in the Spirit, as God, He raised Lazarus from the dead. As a man, He spent nights in prayer; in the Spirit, He forgave sins, answered prayers and performed miracles. In the flesh, He died; in the Spirit, He raised the fleshly tabernacle from the dead.

Hence, when He prayed to the Father, "Not My will, but Thine be done," He was submitting the will of His *flesh* to the will of that *Spirit* that dwelt *within Him* (a phenomenon that presents no problem to believers who also have a measure of the same Spirit of God within them and yet still pray to the God who is Spirit). How can we interpret or even hope to remotely understand such scriptures if not in the above way?

The early Christians viewed Him as God and man, Father and Son, Spirit and flesh, manifested and united in *one* image, *one* body, *one* person: "He is the image of the invisible God, the firstborn over all creation" (Col. 1:15); "For in Christ all the *fullness* of the Deity lives in bodily form" (Col. 2:9); "I and the Father are one" (John 10:30). And because of this oneness in Christ of the human and divine, He can bring fallen humanity to oneness with God, to salvation.

—*The Messianic Incarnation*

Luke 4:22, 33-37; 10:17-20; 6:12; 23:46; Isa. 9:6; John 1:1; 8:19; 2:11, 19-21; 10:18, 30; 11:41, 43-44; 12:45; 14:7-11; Col. 1:19; 2:9-10; Matt. 4:1-11; 8:16, 28-34; 14:15-21; Mark 2:5, 8-10; 7:26-30; 11:12-13; Rom. 1:3; 8:11

Spirit and Flesh

And the Word became flesh and dwelt among us, and we beheld His glory, the glory as of the only begotten of the Father, full of grace and truth.

—John 1:14

And without controversy great is the mystery of godliness: God was manifested in the flesh, justified in the Spirit, seen by angels, preached among the Gentiles, believed on in the world, received up in glory.

—1 Timothy 3:16

As a man, Jesus proved once and for all that the stubborn will of the flesh can come into perfect submission and obedience to the will of the Spirit—to God. Not My will, the will of the flesh, He prayed, speaking as a man to God, but Your will, the will of the Spirit, be done. He was not a man who became a god, which is "the mystery of iniquity," the anti-Christ, the dynamic of paganism; but He was God, the eternal Spirit, who robed Himself in flesh, was found in fashion as a man, "God in Christ," Spirit in flesh, "reconciling the world unto Himself" (2 Cor. 5:19, Ampl., KJV). He was "the mystery of godliness": and "without controversy, great is the mystery of godliness, *God was manifest in the flesh.*"

So, again, Jesus Christ was and is God and man, Father and Son, Spirit and flesh, Bedrock and Foundation, in one image, one body. He is not the second, but He is both the first and the last, the beginning and the end, the Alpha and the Omega, that which was and is and is to come, the Almighty God. As both the Bedrock and Foundation of our salvation, fallen human beings turn

Phil. 2:7; Rev. 1:8, 17; 22:13

unto Him and are saved, for there is no other savior, no, not one.

—*The Messianic Incarnation*

Rev. 1:8; Isa. 43:11; 45:21

The Power of Redemption

The Law had only the power to demonstrate the righteousness of a holy God in *condemning* sin to death. Jesus Christ, however, who came "not . . . to condemn" but to save (John 3:17), has brought "life and immortality" "to light through the gospel" (2 Tim. 1:10): that is, He brought atonement with the immortal source of life through His own death, burial and resurrection. The living, eternal God has revealed Himself in the power of redemption—not in the power of wrath. When He broke through the human wall of fear, Jesus demonstrated that though God is righteous in condemning the world, yet a deeper motive moved Him: He so *loved* the world that He made provision to reveal to humankind His essential nature—His love and mercy. He wanted to bring a people into oneness with the very essence of His Being. That essence is life, not death.

—Garden Enclosed

---

1 Cor. 15:1-4

God's Mercy Unveiled

Nevertheless when one turns to the Lord, the veil is taken away.

—2 Corinthians 3:16

Even though He unveiled it before the eyes of all the world at the cross, God's face of mercy remains shrouded to those bound by unbelief, "veiled to those who are perishing, whose minds the god of this world has blinded, who do not believe, lest the light of the gospel of the glory of Christ, who is the image of God, should shine on them" (2 Cor. 4:3-4, NKJV). To those who turn to Him, however, the veil, the covering, is removed, and as objects of His mercy, they can then behold the riches of His grace shining in the face of Jesus Christ. Through a new and living way, those of faith come to finally see the glory *behind* the veil that has been rent in two. God's true nature has been revealed at the cross.

—A Garden Enclosed

---

2 Cor. 3:16; 4:6; Heb. 10:19-20

Part VII
"My Sheep Hear My Voice"

The Resonance of Truth

My sheep hear My voice, and I know them, and they follow Me.

—John 10:27

To recognize the pitch of the shepherd's voice, one must belong to Him, must stand in or at least be open to an abiding and binding relationship with Him.

—*Truth as Song*

People once called the internal understanding of a design that resonates through the entire universe, but a design that resides in and also can be called forth from deep within us, "truth." And the template of truth within us, along with the depth of our longing to pull its patterns from within us into the light of day where they could correspond with others, determined whether we were "of the truth" or not.

The Esaus are always distracted by other trifling things; but the Jacobs long with everything within them to see whatever truth resides within to be united with God's greater design of an absolute life. Those who are likewise of the truth, when a greater truth comes, will feel whatever bits and pieces of truth that lie dormant within them resonate like a string on one instrument resonates with the string on another when both are tuned to the same pitch. And so this resonant voice of greater truth becomes the voice they follow, and the voice of a stranger they will never follow because of their undying love for this living truth, the only promise of eternal life.

—*All or Nothing?*

Only as we stretch toward the *perfect* man, putting off our individual perspectives to put on the mind of Christ by eagerly submitting to God's order for us within His Body, can we find that proper relationship for all our separate truths.

—*Acknowledging God's Word*

Meaning Comes through Relationship

So our own receptiveness to God's gracious voice, His Spirit-anointed Word, most often as He speaks through the anointed members of the Body, determines whether or not we shall ever perceive and so receive His truths.

—*Taking the First Step: Acknowledgment*

Meaning comes through relationship: we understand a message's meaning because of our relationship with the speaker and because we see how the spoken elements relate to one another and to the one from whom the message comes.

Those who heard but could not understand the meaning of Jesus' words refused to become one with Him. They never knew the total given-overness necessary to experience the depth of feeling from which God's words came forth. They could never, therefore, even hope to see how the authority of God's Word could be both noncompulsory and yet absolute. That such a truth might come to them through human flesh just like their own flesh insulted what they saw as their godlike intelligence. So Jesus' words remained mere meaningless sounds to them.

—*Building Christian Character*

God's Word can never be known "merely conceptually" but must also be seen existentially, "because it affects the whole of human existence." Knowledge of God's Word "is a knowledge more of the heart than of the head, more of

---

1 Thess. 2:13; 1 Pet. 1:10-12; 4:10-11; 1 Cor. 12:4-11; John 12:49-50

the affection than of the intellect. It is a knowledge that causes men and women to tremble."

When we seek to subject the most relational of all forms of communication, God's Word, to detached analysis, we no longer can truly know His Word. When we stop its action upon us and seek instead to act upon it, to smash it in our intellectual and theological cyclotrons, the Word ceases to speak to us as something active and powerful that pierces our darkness with its light.

—Acknowledging God's Word

Isa. 66:2; Jer. 23:9

Two Contrasting Ways of Knowing

The Hebraic perspective reveals two clearly contrasting ways of knowing. The Hebraic way centers knowledge in living relationship with God. It involves an experiential relationship that, in turn, demands the participation of our whole being. In contrast, the pagan way centers knowledge in the lapsed human mind. It involves detachment of the "knower" from that which is "known." The knower analyzes the passive object of his knowledge, generally through an exclusively intellectual objectivity.

—Truth as Song

God's truth is not fragmented and analytically dissolved. Rather, it is brought into interrelationship with our lives as God brings us into deep spiritual relationship with the lives of others and, above all, imparts to us His own life in the Spirit.

—Two Ways of Knowing

Eph. 2:19-22; 4:11-16; John 6:63; 2 Cor. 3:2-6

"That You May Know Him . . ."

And this is eternal life, that they may know You, the only true God, and Jesus Christ whom You have sent.

—John 17:3

Jesus speaks of "eternal life" as a different kind of knowledge—*relational* knowledge, represented by the tree of life. This is a knowledge that brings people *into relationship* with what is called "the living God," and therefore also with other people and creation. This knowledge connects people to God rather than separating them from Him; it brings them *together* with God, with God's people and with God's creation. Coherence and wholeness distinguish this knowledge from fallen knowledge.

—Two Ways of Knowing

The oneness of the Body can alone give expression to truth's living and whole reality, to its relational incarnation of God's love.

—Acknowledging God's Word

John 17

The Scripture Cannot Be Broken

We know that we all have knowledge. Knowledge puffs up, but love edifies.

—*1 Corinthians 8:1*

When Jesus proclaimed that "the Scripture cannot be broken" (John 10:35), the word translated "broken" there is *lysis*, the same Greek root of the word *analysis*. Of course, one kind of breaking down makes God's Word, the living bread, digestible enough to build up the spiritual Body, but another kind of knowledge merely fragments Scripture, killing it and puffing us up in our own knowing.

—*Two Ways of Knowing*

Once the Word is broken, dissolved under the critics' analytical consciousness, it ceases to exist as Scripture. It is like the flower torn apart in order to know it: it no longer exists as a flower.

—*Acknowledging God's Word*

---

1 Cor. 8:1

A New Language

The truth that God's Spirit will lead us into does not merely identify statements about God but rather a whole life that conforms to the image of Jesus and so bears the imprint and fruit of truth.

—Bedrock

When we *see* the patterns and fruit of the Word because we live it, the Word will no longer be a foreign language to us—it will become our native tongue, a language that actually expresses our authentic new birth experience. We will stop simply reading endless menus or recipes and begin to prepare and then eat the meal.

The purpose of the truth is to replant us and then raise us to maturity in the spiritual soil that nurtures us in the Lord, that transforms us into His image. By digging to bedrock, we are seeking to remove everything that would prevent God's Word from being fully effectual in accomplishing His purpose, the purpose of the Spirit, in us.

—Bedrock

"Spirit and Truth"

But the hour is coming, and now is, when the true worshipers will worship the Father in spirit and truth; for the Father is seeking such to worship Him. God is Spirit, and those who worship Him must worship in spirit and truth.

—John 4:23-24

To abandon questions of the truth and authority of God's Word to the desert of rationalistic debates about scriptural semantics that subordinate God's essentially relational Word to abstract human understanding abandons the true purpose and meaning of the Word, for that Word itself insists it can only be understood through what Jesus and Paul described as the leading of the Spirit. In fact, the Word only exists as God's Word when it comes in perfect unity with the Spirit of God, which reveals that Word to human beings relationally.

So while God's anointed, enscriptured Word, as the sole and absolute standard of truth, remains wholly and completely true and free from error, this perfection of His Word can only be seen and understood as it is revealed by the Spirit who authored it. That is, again, Scripture can be understood only relationally, not abstractly.

—Acknowledging God's Word

Certitude in truth comes only when Spirit and Truth stand in perfect consistency and concord. Then, on every level, our whole being testifies that God's presence and God's Word have, in a numinous moment of incomparable awe, united and now resonate together in us. Then our mind

---

John 16:13; 1 Cor. 2:13; 2 Pet. 1:19-21

and heart, our soul and spirit—*everything* within our new nature—tells us that the Spirit and the Word agree as one. As with the men on the road to Emmaus, our hearts burn within us.

—Bedrock, p. 12

God's truth is not fragmented and analytically dissolved. Rather, it is brought into interrelationship with our lives as God brings us into deep spiritual relationship with the lives of others and, above all, imparts to us His own life in the Spirit.

—Two Ways of Knowing

John 6:63; 1 John 2:20-21, 27; 5:6-8; Luke 24:32; Eph. 2:19-22; 4:11-16; 2 Cor. 3:2-6

A Prereflective Sense of Truth

UCLA's Sara Melzer explains that, according to "modern critical theory," what "we perceive as truth is . . . *given* to us *prereflectively* by conventional codes embedded in language."[13] Just as we can hear music because within us inheres a prereflective sense of what music is, a sense reflected in musical scales and tones, so we can perceive truth (if we are "of the truth," acclimated to it) because, just as we are born with perfect pitch, so, too, do we possess, as aphasiacs show, an innate, prereflective sense of what truth is, a sense that our very language reflects.

Jesus Himself specifically linked our ability to recognize truth with a sense of hearing beyond mere words. Thus He declared, "He who belongs to God *hears* what God says" (John 8:47, NIV).

—*Truth as Song*

Hearing the Whole

If you abide in My word, you are My disciples indeed. And you shall know the truth, and the truth shall make you free.

—John 8:31-32

This ability to hear a song is not the ability to hear one part to the exclusion of the rest, but to hear the whole, and so to hear how all the parts beautifully, exquisitely and perfectly come together in composition. When we hear the whole, we hear, then, the Composer, the One who designed the whole and who expresses it through its orchestrated parts, the One of whom the whole is a symphonic expression. To know truth is, then, to hear God. To understand the meaning of each scripture is to hear it in harmony with the meaning and purpose of the whole, as the Composer intended it to shape our lives.

—Truth as Song

Only from the perspective of relational knowledge can facts and theories tie together in such a way as to become relevant to the goals of the God of wisdom. It is only in Him that all things hold together, that the relationships between, and meanings of, facts and theories can be truly seen.

—Wisdom's Children, Book Two

John 8:43-47

Recognizing the Truth

Jesus said to him, "I am the way, the truth, and the life. No one comes to the Father except through Me."

—John 14:6

The song of creation and the words of the gospel go forth and work together, proclaiming the One who is the truth. He has equipped us so that we can recognize His truth, and He has formed our being to resonate in harmony with that truth—if we will open our hearts and believe, fully and *relationally* participating in the Word that comes forth.

To see the truth, we must belong to, bind ourselves to, the One who *is* the truth—not merely some accurate fragment of truth but the *whole* Truth as expressed in the entire life of Jesus, who declared, "I am the . . . Truth" (John 14:6). We must join ourselves to the One who encompasses the whole of eternity and infinity, the One in whom "all things hold together" (Col. 1:17, NIV). Only by our binding relationship with Christ "in whom are hidden all the treasures of wisdom and knowledge" (Col. 2:3) can we hope to see reality in that meaningful perspective that permits us to know and understand the truth. Only God understands the way to "wisdom, and He alone knows where it dwells, for He views the ends of the earth and sees everything under the heavens" (Job 28:23-24, Ampl., NIV). In short, wisdom only comes to completeness when everything is viewed as a whole. And God alone views reality not partially or one-sidedly but with that all-encompassing comprehension that alone can see all interrelationships and so recognize and reveal the full meaning of events, people and things.

—Truth as Song

Acts 14:17

Proper Relationship to the Whole

For since the creation of the world His invisible attributes are clearly seen, being understood by the things that are made, even His eternal power and Godhead, so that they are without excuse.

—Romans 1:20

We can only see truthfully to the extent that we participate in the vision from God that sees as He sees. This is that complete vision which sees the interrelationships between all things.

Researchers explain that notes become music by the way they interrelate, by their *patterns* of relationship. And only when they stand in the proper patterns does a series of notes become music. Apart from that relationship, the fragmented notes merely make noise. Moreover, these notes must relate to the pattern that we recognize as music, a pattern that corresponds both to our innate musical sense and to the pattern lying at the core or essence of all of creation. A note, then, only becomes part of a song insofar as it stands in proper relationship to the whole. Similarly, a fact becomes true, not when simply viewed in isolation, but only when seen in its proper context, in its given relationship to the wholeness that comprises truth.

—Truth as Song

Rom. 1:20-22

A Tangible Experience of God's Love

> *In the beginning God created the heavens and the earth. The earth was without form, and void; and darkness was on the face of the deep. And the Spirit of God was hovering over the face of the waters.*
>
> —*Genesis 1:1-2*

People come into oneness with God only when He lifts them out of their limited worlds into His infinite world of love and mercy, and this cannot happen through a natural act (whether of human emotions, will or mind). Rather, it only occurs through a *supernatural act* of God's power. The actual, tangible experience of God's love is the means He has provided to break us out of our prisons of fallen human finitude, to take us far beyond our finite emotions and minds. Through that experience, God opens up to us the broad vistas of His own understanding, as well as the deep waters of His love as these latter spring forth from His own everlasting life.

In the beginning, God created the heavens and the earth, but this mass of matter and energy remained a formless void until the numinous Spirit brooded over the face of the deep. Through the dynamic moving of the Spirit, meaning emerged from chaos. When in the days of Messiah Jesus first explained to His disciples how they would come into the full understanding of His truth, He told them that the *Spirit* would come to lead and guide them into all truth. The supernatural experience of God's Spirit can alone open human eyes to the meanings of the words He speaks. The Spirit is the Author of those words, and only when He comes and makes His abode within us can we understand

---

1 Cor. 2:4-5; Gen. 1:1-2; John 16:13

the full meaning and truth of that which He has authored.

—Leaving the Lonely Labyrinth

The Ultimate Criterion for Knowing Truth

The Bible itself makes hearing the voice of the Spirit, not linguistics, the ultimate criterion of knowing truth. Therefore, the criterion by which we determine whether or not we have received this Spirit becomes singularly important. If, as some claim, the Bible can only be known and interpreted by seminary-trained scholars, then Jesus apparently made a terrible mistake in choosing to give the keys of the kingdom to a mere fisherman, Peter, or in choosing John as His closest disciple (even as the caregiver to His mother). Moreover, why did He have them pen so many books of the Bible, when Acts 4:13 tells us that "they were uneducated and untrained men"?

—Is Grandpa Saved?

The Voice of the Spirit

Ruling or guiding your life by your own interpretation of this law or that principle, or your own interpretation of this passage or that verse, has only made you lord of your own life. It has done nothing but, at best, bring fragmentation and broken bits and pieces of truth to you, to your family, to the church and to the world. Such approaches of the human mind put themselves in the place of God by piecing together only portions of truth in their own way instead of waiting upon the Lord to build the house by His Spirit. But it's that living voice, that *presentational* reality that transcends your mind, that makes it all effective and therefore makes all the difference. "The Lord is the Spirit," Paul said (2 Cor. 3:17). And no one can say He's really Lord of their life except by the Spirit because if the Spirit is not guiding their life, then the Lord is not guiding their life. In short, Jesus is not their Lord.

It's what that voice, that Spirit, is saying that matters, and how you're obeying that voice determines whether you're part of something that's more than bits and pieces and merely fragmentary representations of truth, a human construct, a mere mechanism, instead of the real and living truth, the Word of God. Oh, yes—He's speaking to us, but do we really hear Him?

—Seeking the Eternal Universal

---

1 Cor. 12:3; Ps. 127:1

Facts without Meaning

The absence of any relationship between facts results in an absence of meaning, but falsely relating facts results in false meanings. Only from the perspective of a transcendent God can facts be related to one another according to their complete and true meaning. Therefore no man "can comprehend what goes on under the sun. Despite all efforts to search it out, man cannot discover its meaning. Even if a wise man claims he knows, he cannot really comprehend it" (Eccles. 8:17, NIV). Only "God understands the way to" wisdom, "and He alone knows where it dwells, for He views the ends of the earth and sees everything under the heavens" (Job 28:23-24). The finite human perspective excludes full comprehension; only God's transcendent perspective—the perspective of the One who "sees everything under the heavens"—enables him to comprehend the total interrelations and meaning of reality. If no such God exists, then humankind is doomed to meaninglessness, destruction and death.

—*Wisdom's Children, Book Two*

The Illusion of Impartiality

The kingdom of God does not come with observation.

—Luke 17:20

Cambridge University physicist Gordon Leslie Squires explained that "an essential feature of quantum mechanics is that it is generally impossible, *even in principle*, to measure a system without disturbing it."[14]

In fact, detached and impartial observation is impossible. Every exalted and detached observer is thus reduced to a lowly and connected participant in what he observes. The observer, in fact, becomes part of the problem to be solved. By the very act of observation and measurement, he colors, shapes, helps determine and always distorts the very outcome of every observation.[15]

—*Acknowledging God's Word*

Changing What Is Possible

According to the most rigorously substantiated research, as quantum physicists study light waves and particles, it has been shown that merely "the decision of an experimenter influences the outcome of an *earlier* part of" his "experiment,"[16] that is, part of the experiment that took place *prior to* the experimenter's decision. In other words, "the [light] particles seemingly 'anticipate' the experimenter's *future* action and alter their trajectories ('teleport') accordingly."[17]

Moreover, small changes in the course of particles in one part of the universe will be perfectly coordinated with changes in another part, even though it is impossible for any energy or matter to reach from one to the other during the time in which the changes take place. The changes happen simultaneously, and this immediate "'adjustment' process" takes place throughout the whole cosmos.[18] Moreover, physicist John Wheeler showed how this process applies to everything and everyone.[19] So every decision a human being makes will affect the entire universe, and even before an individual can put his decision into practice. Professor Jeffrey Satinover claims, for instance, that "what seems to be adjusted is not [always] the precise final outcome of what happens *there*, but rather the *probabilities* of what can [now] occur."[20] This implies that a choice, a decision, made anywhere will change the probabilities of what is possible—in all of creation, in the whole universe.

In another place Satinover says: "In the quantum view, only the broad probabilities are determined; the selection of actual events occurs on a universal scale through some astounding and unimaginable coordination and readjustment of all future probabilities in the light of what actually happens in the present [at this very moment]. Man, on his own small scale, . . . weighs and chooses, a tiny simulacrum—an image—of the larger 'intention' that selects events throughout the universe. Man's choices . . . are taken into account, and the universe is adjusted accordingly."[21]

—Acknowledging God's Word

The Essence of Conviction

Now faith is the assurance of things hoped for, the conviction of things not seen.

—Hebrews 11:1

Just as a marble sculpture emerges amid a heap of discarded chips, we can begin to see what true conviction is by seeing first what it is not. First, the essence of a conviction is not found in what goes on around us. Rather, conviction grows from the seed of God's Word planted within our hearts. The desire to not be left out, or simply to be a part of what's happening, may cause us to do many things, even to radically change our lives to conform to our immediate surroundings, with all their standards, fads or fashions.

Yet such a desire to participate on some vague level in the activities and beliefs of a church community, even one that we may have grown up with but have never authentically been born into spiritually, does not in itself indicate a conviction. We need precisely the *enthusiasm*—literally, "God in us"—that only comes from God's quick and powerful Word piercing us through with its potency and truth, working *in* us by His Spirit to "*will* and to do" (Phil. 2:13).

Of course, the mere exertion of the human will cannot generate the work of God's Word or any authentic enthusiasm; only the death of self-will, followed by the energizing power of God's living Word and coming from God Himself through the Spirit, can do this. We need the Word of God moving not only around us as we stand in the midst of God's people but *in us*, active and sharper than any two-edged sword (Heb. 4:12). It is true that we must actively seek that sword's cleansing work as it cuts away everything from us that settles for mere acquiescence, but we must also recognize that, when it comes, it will not be something we have done but something God has done in bringing us into relationship with Himself.

—Conviction—Possessed by Saving Faith

Constraint Brings Compression

What is not seen as necessary will remain outside the realm of possibility.

—Total Repentance

Like Jesus, we must allow the purpose of God to constrain us to our specific destiny. Constraint brings compression, and compression brings power. Our open-ended options eat away at both our determination and faith like rats on tenement water lines, and so they dissipate the power of God in our life, making for a moldy mess. Because Jesus allowed the purpose of God to completely constrain Him, He spoke with the fullness of God's authority. We, too, must allow God's purpose to completely constrain us, for only then will we have at our disposal the fullness of God's authority and power. If our belief arises from the conviction of God and allows the One who said, "Let light shine out of darkness" to also shine "His light in our hearts," then we, too, can make our declaration with authority: "I believed; therefore I have spoken" (2 Cor. 4:5-6, 13). We can make our confession truly "words to stand by," words of conviction that ring true because *God* has spoken this same clear, precise and unequivocal word into our hearts.

—Conviction—Possessed by Saving Faith

Luke 12:50; Matt. 7:29

One Crucial Truly Free Choice

I have been thinking back to the time when I had finally discovered one truly crucial free choice I really could make: it was the choice as to whether I would *wholly* serve God or simply serve myself. And if I decided to serve God, then the only choice I had to make was whether I would continue to do His will. I've come to see that what we are is what God has given us to be. None of our petty choices matter. Certain kinds of these choices may even seem to vanish when we exert our ultimate—and only real—freedom: the freedom to choose to live wholly for everything transcendent to ourselves, beginning with love, beginning with God. But then what we have, instead of meaningless choices, is gifts. Life, in short, becomes a given. And, then, for the first time we know the real freedom to simply be ourselves, to be what it is a given for us to be.

—*Givens and Losses*

God Hears Your Prayers

Now this is the confidence that we have in Him, that if we ask anything according to His will, He hears us.

—1 John 5:14

Keep praying. You can move the world. You can move heaven and earth when you pray. You may be so weak or tired or whatever that you feel like you can barely lift your voice, but you feel that little unction there squeezing it out of even you, and you begin to pray. It's almost alarming how close heaven starts listening, as if our words are always right next to God's ear. He hears your prayers. He is attentive to the cries rising from His temple. His heart is there.

—Coming into Orbit

Part VIII
"As the First Gleam of Dawn"

Facing Life's Unknowns

Life simply will not conform itself to what we think it should be. A life closed to the unknowns that lie ahead cannot be lived but only endured. It is not life at all. But the realities of life that we face will never bow down in recognition of our godhood. So we will never be able to preplan everything of life, only then joining ourselves to it, secure in our own plans. We can only see and accept the *form* into which an unknown life is to be poured so that the form is always there, a form that can shape our lives into one of meaning and purpose. We can, in short, only learn how to hear God and do what He says. We shall never have the whole of life worked out, along with all of the far-reaching "ifs and ands," the unending ramifications of our choices. All we can ever hope to see is the overall form of the covenant that binds us first to the *living God in His people* and then to the immediate circumstance and situation we face; and within that context, a precise word will come to us at vital moments of great singularity. We must then join ourselves to that word and stand by it until it is fulfilled.

—*Love That Works*

Starting a Spiritual Revolution

And so from this one man, and he as good as dead, came descendants as numerous as the stars in the sky and as countless as the sand on the seashore.

—Hebrews 11:12

God, when He wanted to start a revolution on earth that would turn the whole lapsed world upside down, didn't raise up an army of half a million in Mesopotamia to start the revolution. He called one old man out of the largest commercial city of the area. He asked that old man if he would leave his father, kindred and country and follow the Voice of this unseeable God to an undesignated place. The old man did not even know where he would be going—he had to learn to listen to this unseen Voice in order to even know where he was to go. Then the Voice taught the man to be a new kind of husband and father; He taught the man's wife how to be a new kind of wife and mother. He brought the man into a new level of relationship with Him and kept the man right there by entering a covenant with the man and calling the man His "friend." Then He declared that "Abraham have I known in order that he might command his children after him to walk in the way of Yahweh and do what is right" (Gen. 18:19). Thus did He begin to teach a people about what constitutes the basics of a community of life. And so, because this new form and order for a married couple, for a family, took hold in this man and his offspring, a new spiritual nation, a community of life, unlike any of the coercive polities on earth, was born. And through it, God blessed "all the families of the earth" (Gen. 12:3).

Down through history God has similarly chosen other men to bring spiritual revolution to the world. He always has a man, someone determined, committed, dedicated, nonnegotiable, who will do God's will or die trying. And in this day there will also be key men in key countries who will rise up when God calls and say, "Here am I—send me."

—So You Want Community?

"From Faith to Faith"

God wants to teach us how to walk in relationship with Him. If we truly give ourselves to Him, then we will become more and more accustomed and sensitive to the leading of His love. We begin to learn what we should do and what we should not do. We will begin to sense when God asks us to acknowledge something in our hearts and minds—something in our life—that does not please Him. We therefore become aware of the moments when God tells us to confess when we have done wrong. And we comply with God's desire because we want this close relationship with Him to endure. Nothing must stand in the way or interfere.

We also become aware when God asks us to walk on in greater truths that He unfolds to us so that we might experience ever new levels of His love. And we obey and follow because we know where He is taking us—into the certainty of His presence behind the veil, the veil of human mortality torn open at the cross of Christ. We comply when God asks us to walk on because we love Him; and because we love Him, we trust Him. The more we know Him, the more we love Him; and the more we love Him, the more we trust Him. It is an unfolding journey of love in which "the righteousness of God" is being "revealed *from* faith *to* faith" (Rom. 1:17). So God ever speaks to us, calling us ever closer to Him. And we trust and obey His call, following on in faithful obedience to His leading. Thus do we experience more and more of God's unfolding love and truth.

If we comply and obey on each new level, He will reveal more of His nature, more of His love, more of His righteousness. Then "we . . . with unveiled faces [will] all reflect the Lord's glory, . . . being transformed into His image from glory to glory" (2 Cor. 3:18). This progressive pattern repeats itself until at last we finish our journey. Only then will we be able to say with Paul, "I have finished the course, I have kept the faith" (2 Tim. 4:7). Only then shall we see the Lover of our souls face to face rather than merely through the lattice of mortality, through a glass darkly. Only then shall we be like Him, for we shall see Him as He really is. And only then, at last, will He draw us into His loving embrace forever.

—Experiencing God

---

1 John 3:2

Beyond Our Imagination

Faith is not the denial of reality but the ability to face it.

—The Island

Truth—as the Greek word *alētheia* suggests, which means "unconcealment"—is constantly being unveiled in the unfolding of mystery. The truth is being revealed to us. So we can't cavalierly shoulder our way through life assuming that we know everything, because we certainly don't. Only the smugness and complacency of pride, which more than anything blinds us to the truths hidden in the mystery of life, convinces us that we know everything we need to know to successfully live life. But life has a way of showing us that it's much bigger not only than we thought it was, but also much bigger than we could ever imagine it could be.

—The Mystery of God

Flawed Perceptions

How many times have you looked back on your life at an incident that you saw in one context while it was happening, only to see it five, ten, fifteen, twenty, thirty years later completely differently—so differently that the entire incident has changed in your perspective? That's why I think when some people get older, they become much more qualified in their assessments and their judgments of situations, circumstances and people. You perceive things one way in your youth—or maybe it's not even in your youth—maybe it's when you were getting older, more mature.

But then something new happens, and God speaks from a thick cloud, reframes all our past reality, and suddenly we perceive everything differently than we perceived it before. And it doesn't just mean that we didn't understand the circumstance and situation. Rather, we didn't understand our own heart. We didn't understand our own mind. We could not see what was wrong in us, with that part of us that was doing the seeing in our relationship with reality, with other people. There was something flawed in our way of seeing. The situation actually remains the same, no matter how old we get, doesn't it? Although we do see through earlier flaws of perception, we can't say we see through present flaws of perception that may afflict us now. But because we have changed so much in our perspective, our perspective of our earlier flawed vision becomes greater, more comprehensive, than it was before.

—*The Mystery of God*

Following Christ

Therefore, my beloved, as you have always obeyed, not as in my presence only, but now much more in my absence, work out your own salvation with fear and trembling; for it is God who works in you both to will and to do for His good pleasure.

—Philippians 2:12-13

For Paul, *working out your salvation* becomes a matter of *obedience* in following Christ in the path that He's laid out before us, which "through *death* destroyed him who had the power of death" (Heb. 2:14). The equivalent of a spiritual swoon in magnanimous concession to and pretentious honor of Christ's "wonderful" obedience is not enough: *we* must enter into His obedience by being obedient ourselves, by entering into His death and dying daily. That's why Peter commanded that we must walk in Christ's steps of obedience and suffering in order "that we might die to sins and live for righteousness" (1 Pet. 2:21-24).

—The Preciousness of Death

Luke 9:23-25; 1 Cor. 15:31

Hearts "Set on Pilgrimage"

The path of the righteous is as the first gleam of dawn, shining ever brighter till the full light of day.

—*Proverbs 4:18*

Christians are still pilgrims, still on that march of an unfolding journey from darkness to light, and we will fail to complete our journey unless we raise up a generation that will continue on this path until the full light of dawn breaks forth, until the daystar arises in the hearts of God's people.

Furthermore, the perspective from which man, even a corporate group of people, views reality is partial and limited. Humans as finite beings can never comprehend "the infinite mass" of facts and their relationships. Reality is not merely the sum of its parts but also the subtraction, the multiplication, the division and so much more in the constantly shifting interrelationships of all its parts.

How then can anyone hope to acquire such wisdom? How can anyone hope to realize in their own lives, much less help their children to realize in their lives, this "wisdom that comes from heaven"? First, we must recognize that we do not acquire the full-blown expression of this wisdom all at once. Rather, the Biblical view teaches that this wisdom comes by stages. The path of acquiring wisdom is an unfolding path.

—*Wisdom's Children*, Book Two

Imputation becomes an ongoing, provisional and contingent process, an extension of a line of credit, conditional upon the ongoing impartation through a living and real faith relationship in and with, as well as in obedience to, the sacrifice, the Word and the presence of Christ. And it is indeed Christ who makes all the "payments," but He only does so by depositing more and more of Himself in our lives by His Spirit.

—Total Repentance

Part IX
Strength through Weakness

The Path of Vulnerability

Within the bounds of mutual love given in covenant commitment, we gain courage to open our hearts and make known our own deepest needs as we take responsibility for serving the needs of others. Such a life dedicated to love offers no alternative to vulnerability. After all, life is full of *unknowns*, and to open yourself up to what you do *not* know defines the very essence of vulnerability, of faith in God to lead you on your pilgrimage to a place of relationship you do not yet know, a land of uncertainties that constitutes your entire future life in Him (whether on earth or in heaven).

—*Love That Works*

Necessity Creates Possibility

Now faith is the assurance of things hoped for, the conviction of things not seen.

—Hebrews 11:1

In order to see God do miracles in your life, you must be prepared to make yourself as vulnerable as a mother giving birth to a baby—as vulnerable to risk, vulnerable to pain, to suffering, to failure, to others seeing your weaknesses and vulnerabilities.

Start giving birth to some greater purpose of God in your life, some function in the kingdom that is beyond your present capabilities, some calling transcendent to your known abilities, something that presses you beyond and outside of yourself, and then watch how many people you come into relationship with on a much deeper level than you ever believed possible. It cannot, however, be something that you can now do with a little effort—and so then say, "This is *me*. *I* did it" or, "*We* did this—me and mine!" You may know you have certain gifts or talents appropriate to the task, but you'll see the impossibility somewhere along the way, and you will especially begin to see all that lies within your character, your thinking, your attitudes, that makes it difficult or impossible for the gift to perfectly express or manifest itself in your life. It will be impossible in some way on some level for you.

Praying for the gifts of the Spirit, for gifts of healing and for all the other gifts—it always comes to the place of impossibility and great risk. That's why it's got to be a necessity, a command that comes internally to the soul and settles in as a conviction—something unbacked by any compulsion except the inner compulsion of truth and love—because, otherwise, you won't do what it takes to press forward into

God's grace. When it comes as a necessity, however, you'll know it was the grace of God when you fulfill the necessity.

—*Everyday Miracles*

Fashioning Human Life into Art

It has been a truism, at least in theory, that for 2,000 years the way of Christianity is supposed to be the way of the cross.

How this could be a possibility becomes more understandable by looking at the way one art critic has described the craftsman's work: "Clay is pounded; flax beaten; wool teased, carded and twisted; metal softened and struck. The substance, whether material or human, must change its character, be torn into separate elements in order to be reformed into something other—it must 'die' in order to be 'reborn.' "[22] So, then, from this artist's perspective, the way of the cross would appear to be the *only* way of fashioning (or refashioning) human life into art.

—*What Kind of Family?*

Luke 9:23; 1 Cor. 1:18; Gal. 6:12-14

The Pounding of the Clay

The way of the cross is the way of the artist. Thus did a cabinetmaker's son long ago tell us, "Anyone who does not carry his cross and follow Me cannot be My disciple" (Luke 14:27). This call to the cross was in one sense, then, the call to the discipline of life as art, not an art or a life admittedly of our own creation, but rather, one that shapes us into the given image of the Master Crafter of human lives—the Creator.

When viewed in this way, the adversities, vicissitudes, sufferings and blows of life become not the incomprehensible and unjust workings of blind chance, not a chaotic and absurd source of never-ending perplexity, but the pounding of the clay, the beating of the flax, the carding of the wool, the striking of the metal, the crafting into form, the dying to be reborn.

—What Kind of Family?

Rom. 8:29

"In the House of Mourning"

Everyone faces the carding and twisting, the compressions and reductions, the kneadings and softenings and temperings. They come in the form of physical, mental and emotional trauma and pain and long-term suffering, of accidents and disease and other "misfortunes," of misunderstandings and of strained or even broken relationships, even of persecutions and slander, or of loss of family, friends, home or financial security. Are all these merely the meaningless happenings of time and chance, or are they the blows of the metalsmith's hammer, the poundings of the potter's fist, the cutting by the joiner's chisel? The answer depends on one's attitude, one's viewpoint and the design into which one sees one's life being fitted and configured. If you believe in Marcel Proust's admittedly troubling view, then you believe happiness may be "beneficial for the body," but, in his words, "it is grief that develops the powers of the mind."[23] Solomon, of course, said it long before Proust, and more eloquently, too: "The heart of the wise is in the house of mourning" (Eccles. 7:4).

—*What Kind of Family?*

The Meaning of Suffering

For whom He foreknew, He also predestined to be conformed to the image of His Son, that He might be the firstborn among many brethren.

—Romans 8:29

For Christians, the blows of life are not simply mindless accidents or "injustices" or the arbitrary whim of some impersonal and capricious cosmic force: they are the necessary fashionings of life into the image of God's love and holiness in a world that otherwise can seem at times "without form and void." They are what retrieves meaning from chaos. And so it is the design of both Jesus' individual and corporate life—how all the members of that great family are being related into a meaningful whole—that reveals a *personalized* meaning for each of us in our sufferings. And our sufferings can become, like those of the One whom we claim to be "members" of, a means of realizing Christ's salvation for ourselves and the world.

The question, then, becomes whether or not we have submitted ourselves to *this* design of *this* individual life—the life of Jesus—and have done so by submitting to the design of the larger corporate life over which Christ *now* reigns as Head.

—What Kind of Family?

Rom. 8:29; 1 Cor. 12:12-27; 11:1-3

Yielding to a Greater Design

A key question that comes to mind is whether we will insist on our own design, the invention of ourselves and the conformity of everything and everyone to that design, or if we will at some point finally yield our lesser selves to a greater design. If we insist on our own self-invention, then we are bound to face some tragic disappointments that will no doubt tempt us to blame God, life and everyone and everything else for "letting us down."

If we accept a larger design than one we can invent or imagine, then we can submit to the shaping blows of life that will fit us into the Master Design, a design that the elements themselves cannot always see, since it is so much bigger than they are. But by our acceptance, our surrender, we shall come to know in our hearts that this hard metal of our lives is being heated, softened and pounded for a purpose greater than our selfish ambitions and egocentric indulgences.

—What Kind of Family?

Hidden in the Secret Place

Though the hammer of circumstance may not be swung or the fire of suffering stoked *personally* by God, we have seen them become personalized in the singular life of the crucified Christ who, through love, turned the seemingly blind blows of injustice and human cruelty into the salvation of the world. The same can occur in the context and design of Jesus' corporate life in the community of Christians that calls itself His Body ruled by His very Spirit under His very Headship. So to get inside of this Christ and His Body, or as Paul describes it, to be "fitly framed" into those relationships that "God has composed," is the goal.

When we are reduced enough to fit into such a place, it means our life has been hidden in that secret place where every blow that seems like injustice or brutal (or at least unfair) caprice becomes the hammering blows building the house of our salvation.

—*What Kind of Family?*

Eph. 4:11-16; 2:19-22; 1 Cor. 12:4-12, 18, 24

A Form to Hold the Content of Love

> *But above all these things put on love, which is the bond of perfection. And let the peace of God rule in your hearts, to which also you were called in one body; and be thankful.*
>
> —Colossians 3:14-15

It is the design of the relationships that ties the members of the Body together in God and that thereby gives people the form to hold the content of a love as "strong as death" (Song of Sol. 8:6), a love that "binds . . . all together in perfect unity" (Col. 3:14). It personalizes the hammerings and forgings of life into art by tempering, protecting, covering, forgiving and healing us as we pass through the searing experiences and buffeting blows of self-revelation and behold life—even our own life—revealing itself to us as the art of God. The dismantling of the world we would create for ourselves is often first necessary so that a greater work can take place in our souls to prepare our place in the Artist's house.

—*What Kind of Family?*

A Race between Two Reductions

Life sometimes seems like a race between two reductions. Most know only the reduction of death. They never see that these reductions can be subsumed in the reductions of love. Death reduces by decomposing, tearing apart, fragmenting, destroying the relatedness of all things, the familial order of all life. In some sense, death seems like the ultimate step in a continuum of independence, isolation and finally, the supreme loneliness, or rather aloneness. Love, on the other hand, reduces by continually moving to get the sources of independence and isolation out of the way and then pulling together into a new form all the elements that can hold life. It binds up fragments, heals broken parts and makes whole and obvious the relatedness of everything. It calls us out of isolation, out of selfish independence, and to lose ourselves in a certain *form* of relationship—that of the purest of all possible loves.

When understood from this perspective, marriage and family life comprise one of the great battle stations as love and life conspire against death. They call on first a couple and then a whole family to, in Mike Mason's words, "wholeheartedly, with full consent and . . . joy," enter into "their own diminishment,"[24] to *freely* lay down their lives for love rather than to have life merely dragged away from their little towers of selfishness by the long but inexorable process of "drawing and quartering" that people call death.

—*What Kind of Family?*

Love is not a fantasy that removes us from the struggle of having to live in a lapsed world rife with cruelty, pain, suffering and death—rather, it is a grace that strengthens us in such a way so that supernatural love prevails in life's struggles.

—*Why Build Agrarian Christian Communities?*

Surviving into Old Age

To survive into old age often seems like a process of discovering that what once appeared as the most basic ability to meet our most elemental needs must now slowly, piece by piece, be dismantled and taken away: our youthful vigor, our beauty, our strength, our memory, our health, our friends, our loved ones, our comfortable home, our mental capabilities, our physical mobility, our intellectual and artistic pursuits, our place of work that gave us meaning and recognition, our freedom under law to make our own decisions and choices, even our capacity to eat certain foods or take care of our most essential bodily functions. As Mason so graphically put it: "An old man is a ruined city, a fallen kingdom, a disaster area full of leaks and potholes and crumbling walls . . . . There may be nothing left" of life at the end but "the faintest squiggle on a piece of graph paper"; and "even that may be unceremoniously flicked away like a speck of lint from the collar of the dashing young world."[25]

—*What Kind of Family?*

Beating Death at Its Own Game

Therefore, since the children share in flesh and blood, He Himself likewise also partook of the same, that through death He might render powerless him who had the power of death, that is, the devil, and might free those who through fear of death were subject to slavery all their lives.

—Hebrews 2:14-15

We've eaten of the tree, and, regrettable as it may be, we shall "*surely* die." On one level, life is simply not sustainable in this world. Sadly, this threat looms so huge for some that the inevitable and final loss consumes the whole of their existence; and so they go to their graves "in bitterness, resentment" and even sometimes "rage." Life to them becomes nothing but the ashes of death's reductions because they have never known the reductions of a love that can beat death at its own game and take the heartwood, the invisible soul, of a human being and fashion it into the image of a life of selfless giving, a life that so completely surrenders to love until, when the last blows of death come, nothing remains standing for death to strike except the love against which death has no power.

People who fail to see this alternative miss the vision of love, of the cross as the art of life. So all they can see is the impersonal, insidious, meaningless specter of death as it beats at their door in the middle of the night, frightens them, weakens them, humiliates them, isolates them and knocks out all the supports of their life until, having nothing left to stand on, they simply spin listlessly down the spiraling drain of a dwindling existence in a world condemned to death.

—*What Kind of Family?*

Freedom is "another word for nothing left to lose," nothing that could intimidate us into doing wrong, controlling our lives for larger malevolent purposes and cutting us off from the rule of love.

—*Forming Christ's Body, Book One*

The Transforming Power of Love

Marriage and family are not flights from life's reductions. They simply help us place our reductions in the context of redeeming love, where everything in us that needs diminishment is exposed and confronted so that, in the end, death cannot permanently latch on to us and hold us. Instead, Christians believe that their lives can become hidden through Christ's love in God. In any case, flight or retreat from diminishment is futile, whether we choose love or not. For life's reductions hunt us down no matter where we may run to hide. Marriage and family simply provide one way we can pass through these reductions under the transforming power of love. When we can perceive a great love, not merely in heaven but even reaching down from heaven to incarnate itself on a fallen and diminishing earth, and when we can see that this love can become so powerful that it actually inspires people to lay down their lives for others, it gives us greater courage to turn and face even the ultimate enemy trying to hamstring our souls, until death is swallowed up in the final triumph of God's unfailing love.

So the promise of marriage and family life is that when we suffer, it will not be meaningless—a mere door in space. Even suffering can be sacralized and transmuted when we freely lay down for love—when *we sacrifice*—what we must at last one day lose anyway: we lose what we cannot keep in order to gain what we cannot lose. By doing so, we place our sacrifice in an account that shall never empty because the credit behind it is the unfailing, redemptive love of God.

—What Kind of Family

Love That Cannot Be Canceled

Truly selfless love finally triumphs over death. The collective memory of humankind bears abundant testimony that the lives of those who loved with this love and were loved by it have been far too enriching, too weighty, too wonderful to ever be canceled out by something like death. That is why those who have died in a context of relationships such as that which Christ's Body provides nonetheless continue to live on—through that vulnerable and battered little unit of love called the family, and through that family of families called the kingdom of God, a kingdom into which we're born anew as sons. Generation after generation of those who have gone on—through their prayers and the character they passed on to others—even now rise from their graves and into the hearts and values and beliefs and lives and loves of those who follow the example that they left behind as their works praise them in the gates.

—What Kind of Family?

Prov. 31:30-31

Testimonies of Triumph

Having disarmed principalities and powers, He made a public spectacle of them, triumphing over them in [the cross].

—Colossians 2:15

Solomon said, "Love is as strong as death, and many waters cannot quench it." And John said, "God is love." So what you are surrendering yourself to in your baptism is the laying down of your life at Christ's cross, and you are doing so in love for your brothers and sisters in the context of this Body, this temple of sacrifice, just as Christ commanded. And every time one of God's precious saints dies, the Lord looks down and says, "Oh, how precious in My sight is this death."

This is because every time a true saint dies anywhere in the world, it proclaims to the enemy of all life, "Your power is nothing—I have conquered it again and again through the cross."

Yes, there may have been many struggles along the way, but I have yet to see one of God's saints who didn't go out with the victory, with praise in their heart and words of love on their lips. And what a testimony of triumph that is. The world would call their death a tragedy. But once again, His afflictions are made complete in our sufferings, and so the blood comes streaming down to break the chains of sin and death and set us free. So every time a saint dies in Christ's own victory, another resounding and eternal proclamation goes forth to the rulers and the principalities and powers that "death shall have no dominion," that love will reign *eternally*. That's the course you're committing

Matt. 10:38-39; Luke 9:23-25; Col. 1:24

yourself to when you're "baptized into the likeness of His death." God bless you in the great step you're taking.

—The Preciousness of Death

Far Greater Freedom

For the foolishness of God is wiser than human wisdom, and the weakness of God is stronger than human strength.

1 Corinthians 1:25

How could anyone have guessed that the politically powerless gospel of Jesus, whose adherents never lifted a sword for the first 175 years after His death, but who by the tens of thousands consistently bent their necks to the sword, would become so powerful in its seeming weakness that only when Caesar fused and adulterated it with his own power could it be withstood? It never seemed to occur to anyone at the time that perhaps the Lamb was seeking to release them from a far heavier yoke than Rome's and into a far greater freedom, as well as lead them to a far deeper empowerment.

—*Two Gospels*

God's Purpose for the Church

Christianity can seem to ooze out as a bland but cloyingly sweetened porridge in the midst of prosperity but becomes a sharp and powerful, history-making force in the forge of persecution.

—What Kind of Family?

God purposes that His church should now *unveil* His *life* to the world; and only the living membrane, the bond of love, transparent to the entrance of light, can in turn reflect the glory of God. Through our vulnerability, our weakness, the very fragility of the membranes of life, the surpassing strength of His love will shine through and triumph over brute force. Jesus tells us, therefore, to no longer respond with an "eye for an eye," even though this law may be just for the world. We can no longer defend ourselves with the external might and power of the arm of the flesh, for we who have received mercy now stand obligated to mercy.

—A Garden Enclosed

Part X
Repentance unto Life

Grafted into the Root

Repentance races judgment in laying the ax of truth at the *root* of the tree of our old nature. If it wins the race, then it extirpates our life from a culture of infallen death. It does not merely lop off a few of the dead limbs. It does not merely deal with the *symptoms* of the ailment, futilely trimming and pruning here and there. Rather, it goes to the *source* of the disease. It cuts away at the very root of our old existence, our old habits of thinking and behaving and the old merely human culture that sustained and nurtured them. It does this so that we might be grafted into the tree of indestructible life found only in Christ. Jesus was Job's new tree: He was the sprout that sprung forth through the womb of Mary, from the dead stump of humankind cut down at the Fall. He is the "root and the offspring of David" (Rev. 22:16), the root that sprang forth out of dry ground. In the midst of the spiritual aridity and sterility of a world of religious "dead works," Jesus Christ came forth as a living root from the ground of God's very Being. That root became a vital vine into which we must be grafted.

—The Turning Point

Prov. 3:18; Col. 2:2-3; Job 14:7-9; Isa. 53:2

Becoming Centered in Christ

There are two centers that may be chosen: one, the human, immanent, material and natural center; or, two, the divine, transcendent, spiritual and supernatural center.

—Wisdom's Children, Book Two

Like falling water, individuals are ever inclined toward self as the center. Everyone must undergo certain demolition steps through which each dies to his own center, uprooting himself from the death-bound, egocentric perspective that claimed our first ancestor and that has been passed down from each succeeding generation to us.

Such a shift in centers is no minor or whimsical matter. In fact, it is the most difficult of all changes people ever undergo. We can even say that it's analogous to dying, since virtually *every* natural inclination in us opposes making Christ or anything else but ourselves the center.

—The Turning Point

Seeking Transparency

If we refuse to chisel away everything not of Him, we can never be conformed to His image.

—Forsaking Sin

Repentance is dying to all our man-made images, no matter how religious they seem. Repentance is consciously offering up those images unto God. And so we pray, "Oh God, shatter this image of self-righteousness. Bring me to a place of transparency. Carry me past merely what's 'appropriate' in human eyes, and let me feel *Your* heart in receiving *Your* gift and then in passing it on. Let me be transparent. Let me be free with my heart, with the love You have given me."

—Bedrock

This "repentance unto acknowledgment of the truth" also, then, means taking the extremely difficult step of a tearing down, a divestment, of all of our illusions about ourselves, life and the world. It follows that our source of information about such things can no longer be the fallen world and all its endless, biased views, but only God Himself. We will no longer worry constantly, or only, or even primarily, about what people think of us or how they define reality, but rather, we shall now become focused on knowing the mind of God.

—Taking the First Step

Repentance Brings Acknowledgment

And the tax collector, standing afar off, would not so much as raise his eyes to heaven, but beat his breast, saying, "God, be merciful to me a sinner!"

—Luke 18:13

To truly serve God, we must discard all doctrines that settle us into the complacency of fallen human flesh. We must instead fall upon the Rock of the living Word in order to allow God to break through every barrier of pride and allow our will to be broken to His will as expressed through His corporate Body on earth, the Body He prepared to do His will. No decision that we come to in life will be more agonizing and cause us more soul struggle than this one. In the end, only the deepest sort of travail, a desperate and heart-rending prayer acknowledging fully our sin, confessing it completely, begging God's forgiveness with tears and weeping that arise from the very depths of our soul, and then forsaking our sin, can bring us to this place of total brokenness to the will of God.

An authentic repentance brings acknowledgment of the truth about ourselves as our inner motives and intentions are laid bare by and revealed to us through the piercing light of God's living Word, often coming prophetically through those sent to minister to us insights that reveal the secrets of our hearts.

—Taking the First Step

Heb. 4:12; 10:5-7; 1 Cor. 14:24-25

Acknowledging Harder Truths

> *The first step of repentance tears down and uproots the old fallen thought-edifice of our life—the life bound for death. Scripture speaks of several elements involved in this tearing-down process: "acknowledgment," "confession" and "forsaking."*
>
> —Taking the First Step
>
> *God perhaps will grant them repentance to acknowledging of the truth.*
>
> —2 Timothy 2:25

Acknowledgment of the truth means allowing God to penetrate through and expose all of our false images, ambitions, aspirations and dreams, whether our illusory dreams have been manufactured in Hollywood or Harvard, in Woodstock or Washington, D.C., whether we see ourselves as characters from *Ivanhoe* and *Little Women* or from *The Green Berets* and *Dirty Harry* or from *The Color Purple* and *The Feminine Mystique* or the *New Yorker*, the *Wall Street Journal* and Madison Avenue. We must deeply desire (not merely reluctantly acquiesce) to surrender every image and ideal that finds anything of its origins outside of God and His Word. We must not only allow but also even seek God's shaking of everything that can be shaken.

A perhaps still harder truth to acknowledge is the truth about ourselves. Many are ready to receive, acknowledge and even search out the most penetrating and ugly truths about the qualities and characteristics and notions and ideas and beliefs that they dislike both in other people and in the world that lies outside their own private world. They become excellent judges of everything but them-

---

Heb. 12:25-27

selves. Of course, the capacity to come to God hinges on our ability to accept the full truth about *everything*, but most especially ourselves: *our* worldview, *our* religion, *our* traditions, *our* lifestyle, *our* relationships, *our* habits, *our* ideas, *our* attitudes, *our* motives, *our* behavior, *our* character, *our* cherished beliefs, *our* social status, *our* familial and ethnic roots and ancestry. Repentance begins first of all with these; and if it doesn't begin here, then it never fully materializes.

In short, failure to make a complete acknowledgment will ultimately bring us to ruin.

—*Taking the First Step*

Ceasing from Excuses

If we cannot accept responsibility for our participation in original sin, we cannot receive the possibility of participation in Christ.

—Forsaking Sin

We naturally see all our problems as lying in the stimulus to sin, not in the response—not in us. Therefore, we merely become slaves to sin. Whatever stimulates us and tells us what to do—that determines how we respond. We are then controlled, mastered, by something outside ourselves; and it is sin that has gained this mastery over us.

If you bear no responsibility for what has supposedly befallen you out of nowhere, then you also have no power of remedy. For one can only hope to become responsible, to overcome his failures, by recognizing his own personal responsibility for these failures.

If we want victory, then we must stop excusing, justifying and defending ourselves; we must stop blame shifting like Adam did in the garden. We must recognize our need to be totally restructured into God's temple according to His blueprint and pattern. When we *fully* recognize this, and commit to utterly change our behavior accordingly, the old habits *will* die. Then God will rebuild us if we'll continue to walk in transparent consciousness of Him, stepping into His light faithfully and obediently on a day-by-day, moment-by-moment basis, acknowledging and confessing our sins and mistakes each and every time they arise, cutting them off at the first hint of their appearance. If we do this consistently, God will work a change and create His new image in us. Old things will pass away, and all things will be made new.

—*Taking the First Step*

2 Cor. 5:17

Cutting Off Sin

If your hand causes you to sin, cut it off. It is better for you to enter into life maimed, rather than having two hands, to go to hell, into the fire that shall never be quenched.

—Mark 9:43

God's feelings about sin remain to this day "unsparingly" the same, for He is the Lord who changes not. He holds no quarter with, and gives no compromise to, sin; and He insists that His people do the same. He commands us to bind the strong man of the sinful nature, to bring its every thought into captivity to the mind of Christ. He gives us this command because only *this complete commitment* to resist evil will effectively defeat it. Anything less only invites the ultimate defeat of our own soul.

Such a decision, a cutting off, is, of course, impossible for a mind that still doubts the necessity of action. Necessity is lost in the misty clouds of doubt, of self-rationalization and justifications, of obscurity and confusion and all the vague areas where no authentic or real "cut" has even been made.

Therefore, cutting off sin means somehow exchanging our own headship over our lives for the Headship of Christ, our own mind for Christ's mind; and this is done by surrendering our minds completely to the control of the Spirit.

—*Forsaking Sin*

Mal. 3:6; Matt. 12:29; 2 Cor. 10:5

Dying to Double-Mindedness

No one can repent with a mind only half made up, because repentance is itself death to the will of the carnal mind, and death is not a partial phenomenon. Nothing is so final and complete.

—Total Repentance

James gives us the cure for double-mindedness: "But He gives a greater grace. Therefore it says, 'God is opposed to the proud, but gives grace to the humble.' Submit therefore to God. Resist the devil and he will flee from you. Draw near to God and He will draw near to you. Cleanse your hands, you sinners; and purify your hearts, you *double-minded*. Be miserable and mourn and weep; let your laughter be turned into mourning, and your joy to gloom. Humble yourselves in the presence of the Lord, and He will exalt you" (James 4:6-10, NASB).

These last sentences do not express what most would call a "happy" experience. They express a "demolition," a "tearing down" of an old way of feeling and thinking. A revolution is not a happy event. It must be paid for with great sacrifice, great anguish and great cost as God uses the circumstances of life to tear down everything of the flesh in which we trusted. But revolution does liberate, and that is part of the joy set before us as we endure the cross of sacrifice.

Repentance is saying, "I am *willing* to begin my walk with God; I am ready and eager to begin walking in the path of obedience to His commandments as His Spirit leads me. I am willing and eager to begin to 'follow on to know the Lord,' and I have made up my mind now and forever to do so."

So repentance is all about dying to the control of self-will, of lapsed "flesh." It initiates a life lived unto the Spirit and will of God. Through repentance we die to our double-mindedness. We die to our belief in and reliance upon the superiority and self-sufficiency of the fallen human mind and the dying body to which it's attached. We die to the human-centered, pagan, naturalistic, objectivistic, humanistic thinking of rationalism, relativism, hedonism, individualism and materialism that sunders each soul within himself, that severs him from his fellow man, from God's world and from God Himself.

—*Total Repentance*

Breaking Self-Will

*For You do not desire sacrifice, or else I would give it;
You do not delight in burnt offering. The sacrifices
of God are a broken spirit, a broken and a contrite
heart—these, O God, You will not despise.*

—Psalms 51:16-17

The breaking of the human will to the will of God stands as the ultimate goal of repentance. While all other perfections may still seem out of reach, the perfection of will is one of the only perfections fully attainable for even the newest convert. And when the will is fully and permanently determined to completely submit to God's will—this is when a true Biblical repentance has taken place.

Our will does not then vanish. It is always there. Yet it must be broken in its resistance so as to willingly and eagerly conform to His will. Since God will never force our will, only a superhuman love can accomplish this goal.

—Bedrock

A Made-Up Mind

A made-up mind is a mind dead to every lapsed authority and desire but God's, even its own. Jesus is truly Lord of such a life.

—Total Repentance

God does not ask us to make a step-by-step "reformation" in regard to any particular sin. He demands a total and complete transformation, a severance, "a cutting off." It is not a slow, gradual process whereby we leave sin a little at a time like a patient "drying out" from heroin in a methadone clinic. This gradual approach only says that someone has failed to truly make up their mind; they have not come to a place of total commitment, of cutting off all the options to sin.

So the severance from sin can only be done with a *totally* made-up mind. Nothing less is true repentance. Nothing less works, and nothing less will bring the desired results in our relationship with God and His people.

—Forsaking Sin

Digging to Bedrock

Therefore whoever hears these sayings of Mine, and does them, I will liken him to a wise man who built his house on the rock.

—Matthew 7:24

Builders seeking places to build the foundations of towering buildings in great cities often come across the ruined foundations of buildings that once stood there. Sometimes they hit something that at first seems solid, perhaps old stonework and collapsed fragments of brick walls. They *could* theoretically start building there, but eventually their new building would topple because their foundation would eventually shift, only *seeming* to have solid footing but still not standing on bedrock.

Believers, however, must clear away *everything* of a lapsed and human-centered past, clear it completely out of their hearts and minds, no matter how seemingly solid and good it may appear. We must dig until we stand on nothing but the solid Word of God expressed to us by God Himself. If something of the past is indeed good, then God will establish or restore it *in its proper order*. But no house that falls short of planting its whole foundation upon the living encounter of the Word of God in the living relationship of the Body of Christ through which God speaks will ever be able to endure in standing against the adverse conditions that arise in a fallen world and in the course of every human life.

With any foundation, the answer is determined by the type of terrain to be built upon and the type of structure to be built. Since our structure will stand as God's eternal temple, we must dig until we strike bedrock. Only bedrock provides a strong enough underpinning for this foundation.

In the first step of repentance, demolition, we have, through acknowledgment, confession and forsaking, freed ourselves by God's grace from that which would prevent us from moving into this relationship with God's Spirit and His own corporate Body. Now we begin to dig until we tangibly touch bedrock, laying the necessary groundwork for an experiential relationship with the Spirit as well as with the people within whom the Spirit dwells as the corporate habitation of God.

—Bedrock

Eph. 2:22

An Ongoing Need for Humility

Humble yourselves in the sight of the Lord, and He will lift you up.

—James 4:10

Humility speaks of an attitude toward ourselves, others, the world and God: it means that we no longer move in blithe unawareness and unconsciousness of God in the everyday moments and deeds and idle words and self-indulgences of our lives.

This humility of mind is how we forsake sin. If all this seems impossible, it only shows our need to depend upon, to lean heavily and constantly upon, the Holy Spirit and the grace of God. It means, in other words, that we cannot live unto ourselves but that we must learn what it means to daily humble ourselves before God in acknowledgment of our moment-by-moment need of Him.

—*Forsaking Sin*

Dying Daily

When we repent, we die to the death inherent in us.

—Bedrock

Our will can fully break to God's only when and if we come to face God and our full responsibility for every failure, problem and shortcoming in our lives. We have broken only when our will has died to the death-nature within us. When we die this death to egocentricity and break fully on bedrock, we must then stay firm in our commitment to that death to death. Even after we have fully committed our will to put the old lapsed nature to death, after we have begun to tear down the *old* rotted structure, still the old habits of mind and thought, of attitudes and ways of relating to people and situations, will attempt to again gain mastery over us.

We must tell ourselves over and over, in every confrontation, "It doesn't matter what happens here to me. It doesn't matter if I am going to be taken advantage of. Nothing matters, because I'm dead to this whining dead man. I pledged it, I vowed it, I made a covenant to seal it. In repentance I have put the old corrupt nature to death in God's name."

So we have entered a struggle, joined in a battle; and we must *daily* pick up our cross and follow Jesus, crucifying the carnal man each time it would rise up again to tempt us, saying to ourselves, "Death, you are dead." Merely *fighting* and thrashing around in this battle in the flesh will not work. We must sacrifice. We must pray. We must search God's Word. Only the death of death will work. Then we will have the abiding sense that our real life is truly hidden with Christ in God. If we let a little slip by here and then a little more there, finally we will be *bound* by the old patterns and habits again, *slaves* to sin. We must put our old nature to death *daily*, recognizing it as a culprit deserving death. Otherwise, according to the Lord's own words, we pronounce ourselves unworthy to be Jesus' disciples.

—*Total Repentance*

Col. 3:3; 1 Kings 11:1-11; Matt. 10:38

Dying to Death

When we put the sinful nature to death, we die to the principles that bring disintegration and divisiveness to our lives. We instead begin to live for that which brings cohesion, purpose and meaning. Again, in short, life comes forth only as we begin to die to death. Spiritual life follows carnal death. So we must die to the way of thinking that cuts us off from love, from life, from each other, from God. Without this death to self and its world, we have no hope of peace, joy or an experienced reconciliation with God.

Similarly, the laying of the temple foundation must begin with a negative step because something already stands on the life site of each one of us—an old, rickety and dilapidating structure that must be completely demolished and destroyed. This negation describes what repentance is all about. Yet, again, what it finally negates (as Hebrews 6:1 informs us) is actually only the ultimate of all negations—death. In repentance, in short, we die to death.

—Total Repentance

The Acceptable Sacrifice

I beseech you therefore, brethren, by the mercies of God, that you present your bodies a living sacrifice, holy, acceptable to God, which is your reasonable service. And do not be conformed to this world, but be transformed by the renewing of your mind, that you may prove what is that good and acceptable and perfect will of God.

—Romans 12:1-2

Only through our own breaking in repentance will God show us that His will is expressed through a Body of like-broken people and their like-broken leaders, a Body over which He alone has the preeminence. Such an experience may take place just about anywhere. But wherever and whenever it occurs, it must be thorough; it must be complete. It must leave us with a sense of being willingly and even joyously shattered on God's absolute sovereignty for our lives. Only then can we look up to see that other stones also stand upon this same bedrock.

In other words, something within the lapsed human nature stumbles any time God's Word comes to it, and this something that stumbles is *apeitheia*, the refusal to be "fully persuaded" that the Word that comes to us is coming from God and means exactly what it says.

This temple, then, is the place where we must go to offer up our acceptable sacrifice. This acceptable sacrifice is not something we offer up from our carnal lives; rather, God wants the sacrifice of our lives: He wants us to say with Jesus, "I have come to do Your will."

—Bedrock

Deut. 12:1-5; Rom. 12:1-3

Dead Works Bear Plastic Fruit

Therefore bear fruits worthy of repentance . . . . And even now the ax is laid to the root of the trees. Therefore every tree which does not bear good fruit is cut down and thrown into the fire.

—Matthew 3:7-8, 10

Some people—hating the death, the digging, the dunging, the pruning that comes with repentance—have supposed that even the *fruit* of the Spirit could be achieved by superficial "dead works." So on the table of the Lord, spread with precious living fruit, also stand examples of those who express only the plastic fruit that merely *appears* to be loving, joyful, peaceful, patient, kind, good, faithful and so on.

The failure to die in repentance, then, is evidenced by the "dead works" of a dead, fruitless faith. Living fruit must come from a living tree.

—*Total Repentance*

Luke 13:8

Discipling Relationships

Without relationships based on the principles of Biblical discipleship, we cannot consistently uproot the carnal nature from our lives.

—Forsaking Sin

If we truly want freedom from sin, we must seek out relationships that will bring the arrow to full draw and unswervingly aim God's Word at the root of sin. At the same time, the form of those spiritual relationships holds the carnal nature in check, restraining it, putting it to death as they help mortify the deeds of the flesh.

So it is precisely our confession that Jesus has come in the flesh that enables us practically, in our day-to-day experience, to cut off sin, to overcome temptation and to put the carnal nature to death in all the concrete particulars of our lives.

—Forsaking Sin

Those who freely and truly commit to join themselves to God enter into a marriage covenant with Him. This means, first of all, that such people have committed to fling aside these barricades of the sinful nature, barricades that separate them from God. And they have determined not only to give His Spirit and His anointed Word *unlimited* access to their lives, but also even to actively seek out a total surrender of those lives.

—Taking the First Step

Ps. 2:1-3; Rom. 6:1-18; 8:1-13, 29; Isa. 62:1, 5; John 3:27-30; Heb. 12:22-23; Eph. 5:22-33; 4:22-24; 2 Cor. 11:2; 3:18; Rev. 19:7-9; 21:2; 22:17; 1 Cor. 15:49

Repentance is, then, the spiritual phenomenon that prepares our hearts for sonship. It turns us in brokenness and submission to a network of relationships that allows us to receive fully the training, the discipleship, of the Father as He brings His loving authority to bear in our lives through His Body.

—Total Repentance

Resurrection Power

The death, burial and resurrection of Jesus is the "good news" that God made a way to restore a believing people to their place as His spiritual habitation, breaking satan's hold over all those who are found "in Christ," who walk in the light of the Word.

—The Turning Point

This resurrection power isn't an add-on that comes to us at the last moment of our complacently, casually and carelessly lived lives; God intends this power to pervade our lives in ever-increasing measure as we live for and serve Him by laying down our lives in daily service for our brothers and sisters. To truly lay down our lives, we must give up our own ambitions, plans, comforts, convenience, images, dreams, desires—everything that we seek for ourselves. As we die to all this, He replaces them with His own plans and purposes that bring a fulfillment, meaning and peace beyond anything we could ever have acquired for ourselves.

—Total Repentance

Part XI
"I Will Not Leave You Orphans"

Explanation over Experience?

> *I count all things to be loss in view of the surpassing value of knowing Christ Jesus my Lord . . . that I may gain Christ, and may be found in Him, not having a righteousness of my own derived from the Law, but that which is through faith in Christ . . . that I may know Him and the power of His resurrection.*
>
> —*Philippians 3:8-10*

Explain music to someone who has never heard a musical note. Explain color to someone blind from birth. Explain the poetry of your mother tongue to someone foreign to the language, or who knows not a word beyond the prosaic and the technological. Just so, neither can anyone explain God coming in the immediacy of His presence to those who have only at best vaguely heard *about* Him. Some may, of course, have even mastered theological studies, concepts, creeds or theories *about* Him, but these are almost as distanced from a direct encounter with God, or a moment of experienced relationship with Him, as the mathematics of genetic combinations is from the love and marriage that brings forth children.

—*On the Holy Spirit*

Experiencing the Numinous

In the 1920's a German professor of theology, Rudolf Otto, wrote of what he saw as a serious need for something beyond merely religious institutions, organizations and dogmas, something more than words and concepts. Somewhere God Himself needed to be present, but European churches, in Otto's view, failed to present such a God.[26]

Otto, facing this problem in the '20's just before the collapse of Christian culture in Germany, coined a new word to describe what was missing (a word now found in almost any English dictionary). The original word was *numen* (from the Latin), and from it he extrapolated the word *numinous*. Yet to this word he attached an altogether new meaning, one that went far beyond anything suggested by the Latin root: to Otto, it became the awe-inspiring presence of the supernal as it overwhelms all human thoughts and words, even overwhelming the whole schema of a merely humanly generated reality.[27]

A problem arose, however, that prevented most people from having such an encounter: when they came in contact with this living reality beyond mere words, beyond even doctrine, when they directly encountered the divine Presence Himself, something seemed to fill them with dread—not a common dread but a holy and transcendent dread. And it seemed to come upon them precisely *because* they were experiencing something so *un*common, so *extra*ordinary, so moving, so transcendent to their physical life and the natural, material, immanent world in which they were situated. In other words, it was so numinous, and people were so natural; it was so Other, and they were so situated in time and matter, in natural relationships. So they could not fit it into any mode of what constituted their habitual thinking patterns.

This sense of an inexplicable dread, of a power *too* full of numinous love, *too* holy and transcendent, and therefore incomprehensible, ultimately seems to lie behind the many theological confusions that attempt to "flatten out," in Otto's words, our sense of the direct presence of God. In short, such theology helps us bottle God and put Him under our control, make Him less overwhelming, more mentally manageable. At the same time, this understanding gives us a clue as to when we can know that the Holy Spirit might be breaking in upon our experience in a visitation of numinous power.[28]

—*On the Holy Spirit*

An Unveiling

The first step into an experience of God comes in the initial awareness of God's presence in our own lives. From the start, a powerful soul stirring is followed by a great turning point in an individual's existence. This is not merely a self-motivated reformation based on the arid assent of the human intellect—it is a God-motivated transformation based on an encounter with the *mysterium tremendum*, the divine and personal ground of all being.

Perhaps God's most powerful act to bring us to such a turning point is the deeply emotive evocation of the direct moving of His Spirit upon us. When God speaks to us through such a powerful manifestation of His own nature, it reveals to us how far short we have fallen from our full potential for joy, peace and love—how far short we have fallen from the perfect pattern for our life that God Himself has not only given but also personified in the life of Messiah. We suddenly see and experience the reality of God in a spiritual unveiling of overwhelming magnitude and power. When we then compare our own condition to God's perfection, we feel humbled—even ashamed. At this point, we may often at first only want to flee from such a vision, trying to hide ourselves and deny all of our imperfections and shortcomings. This, of course, proves ultimately impossible; and even if it were possible, it cannot help us. Such an apocalypse, an unveiling, can occur either now in our repentance or later in judgment. But occur it surely will.

So revolutionary is the experience of turning to God that it's truly like stepping into a different world: a different way of seeing, of thinking, of knowing, of living, of loving. And indeed, it represents the first steps into the parallel universe of God. Awed and amazed, for the first time, an individual soul begins to see through just an infinitesimal fragment of the vision of God, to feel with some minute part of the heart of God and to understand and know even some quark of the mind of God. But such crumbs from the table of the eternal only drive us deeper and deeper into this unending source of everything beautiful, true and good.

—Experiencing God

Beyond Mere Religion

You will show me the path of life; in Your presence is fullness of joy; at Your right hand are pleasures forevermore.

—*Psalms 16:11*

No life touched by a powerful and transforming experience with God's Spirit will ever be the same after this turning point. Everything else in the world will seem as unreal as a child's playhouse. A sense of cleanness sweeps over those who have this experience. It makes them desire to shed their old lives—their old way of thinking, feeling and living. So great will be His love that it seems to people as if they have never loved or been loved before. So great is the experience of His truth that it seems as if all previous truths were but lies and deception. So great is the experience of His goodness that mere human goodness may seem more like evil. So great is His experienced life that all that we have ever lived before is seen to fall under the grim shadow of death.

Those who have this experience can scarcely believe they have actually entered into what they are indeed experiencing. Yet so real, so beautiful, so perfect will it be that if it were a dream, they would immediately give their life just to go on dreaming. They would willingly give everything they have ever known, experienced or possessed just to feel the breath of this God breathing deep into their souls. Nothing will matter at that moment except that God is there, that He is real, that He cares and that He knows each of us for what we are and yet loves us enough to empower us to become what He sees we can be in Him. So real is His friendship that we would surrender every friendship to feel what we now feel. So far beyond mere religion is this *experience* of love that all human-centered religion seems left behind in the stale past forever. Our only desire is for the immediacy of God and His guidance into the fullness of His truth.

—*Experiencing God*

In the Cool of the Day

This is eternal life, that they may know You, the only true God, and Jesus Christ whom You have sent.

—*John 17:3*

At some point along our journey of faith, we become acquainted enough with God to discover that He has a personal name—Jesus. We soon see that Jesus was and is the fullest expression of God ever to appear on earth—in fact, He is God's Spirit robed in human flesh. So when we look into the face of this Jesus, we gaze into the glory of God. He is the "exact representation" of God's very "being." No one walked in the truth and love of the God named Yahweh like Jesus did. His very name means, "Yahweh has become salvation." Jesus is the irradiated "brightness of God's glory." That's why His name can become so deeply a part of us that we call upon it for every need. When lonely or troubled, we escape to our secret garden of prayer and begin to call upon the name of the new Lover of our soul.

The world wonders why we quietly remove ourselves to our garden, but we know that when we enter into this secret place of the Most High, He will be there. He responds to the call of His name, draws near to us, knowing that we are His and that we have reserved ourselves for Him and none other. There, in the cool of the garden, we reenter into a communion with God, a communion that man and woman once walked in so long ago. We talk with God and share in all the highest dreams and hopes of the ages, seeing them realized for the first time in our own lives.

Yes, He beholds us through the lattice of mortality. He looks upon us through the windows of the temporal, calling us further still, beckoning us on to leave it all and run with Him on the pathways of the eternal—even on those paths lined with trouble, hardship, pain, misunderstandings, persecution and death. He tells us how He walked the same road before us and how He struggled His way up the dusty road to Death's Head to take His final steps into God's perfect love. He beckons us to prepare ourselves that we might soon join Him in that world of unending love, peace and joy.

—Experiencing God

"Yes, God, Yes"

When God's Spirit descends upon you in a living, visceral reality and you experience His love as it vibrates over your body, in the cells of your mind, inside the deepest part of your soul, and you know—because you *experience* it—that it's God, then suddenly all of life seems simplified. Everything seems small and insignificant in the magnitude of that moment.

God becomes more real than your closest friend, than your own family, than the breath you breathe, than you yourself—more real than even the world around you. You hear Him, sense Him, feel Him and absorb Him into every part of your being. The presence of His love suffuses you so powerfully, so completely, that everything negative washes away in the welling up of that Spirit throughout your mind, body and soul. And everything within you begins to say, "Yes, God, yes."

—Experiencing God

Spirit and Truth

But the hour is coming, and now is, when the true worshipers will worship the Father in spirit and truth; for the Father is seeking such to worship Him. God is Spirit, and those who worship Him must worship in spirit and truth.

—John 4:23-24

Jesus said that *the Holy Spirit* (not any pyramidal human hierarchy) should lead and guide us "into *all* truth" (John 16:13), and that the "promise" of the Holy Spirit was to carry us into "the very *certainty* of the Presence within the veil" (Heb. 6:17-19, Ampl.)—in short, that God Himself, through the Holy Spirit, can and would provide the certainty we all long for.

Of course, I'm not assuming that the Holy Spirit never leads those who come together in church councils or works *through* the church—I'm only assuming that individual believers must also have their own genuine relationship with that same Spirit before they can ever experience as individuals the authentic certainty from God, a certainty they claim to long for when looking at the multitude of confusing options that today go forth in the name of truth. Otherwise, how could they ever hope to discover with any certainty for themselves which local church, or even which church council, God was confirming as the context in which to disciple them in obedience to the truth?

To separate the experience of God's Spirit from the revelation of His Word is to separate the expression of God, His Word, from God Himself, from His presence, from His Spirit as expressed through His true Body. And (to be candid) this seems to meet the requirements of a sound definition of idolatry—that is, given that your faith must rest on *someone's* understanding and interpretation of "the rock of God's Word," even if only your own.

—*On The Holy Spirit*

Theology or Relationship?

Just as we can stand unseeing in front of a painting, so can we stand in the presence of God's Spirit, yet our experience of it will remain relatively untransforming because the depth of our participation falls short.

—Building Christian Character

Those who have best promoted a real knowledge of God have seldom appealed, at least at the outset, to theoretical considerations and judgments. Neither have they spoken overmuch of "sources" for their theories. As one writer has said, "The water must be fetched and drunk fresh from the spring if it is to flow through us at all," if it is to quicken our own hidden sources. Yet here, too, "there's many a slip between the cup and the lip," and by the time we get to the spring, we've met a dozen hawkers pushing their stale bottled water and warning us to "watch out" for the spring.

A true knowledge of God, an actual experience of His presence, has become so completely alien to many today that, far from even considering that we might seek such an experience, most feel it a necessity, instead, to pause and consider not only the uses that such knowledge has posed but also the individual's possible attitude toward such an experience and all its attendant risks. It even seems likely that we may have been all too well inoculated against any direct relationship with God by our small and unaffecting doses of theology merely *about* God. This reduction of God to a mere idea or concept has caused us to lose even the possibility of feeling our way toward the great and immediate realities of the Spirit that invaded and transformed human experience and human lives some two thousand years ago at the birth of Christianity.

—On the Holy Spirit

A Demonstration of Power

The vaccine which produces our own spiritual loss today is precisely our all-too-willing, helpful and efficient "science of God"—our God-in-a-bottle theologies. Such bottle theologies have so well explained (or, better yet, explained away) the drink in the cup that we have become sure we know all about it even before we've touched our lips to it.

In fact, we are sure we know far better than the good old "drinkers" in the days of the apostles Peter and Paul (and of Mary, too, according to Luke's record in Acts 1:14; 2:1-4). And so we have come to rest content with our "knowing better" or even to rate our abstract mental knowledge as higher than any unspoiled experience or direct joy in the whole-souled presence of God Himself. "Don't exalt experience of God above the Word of God" is the mantra we chant to ourselves—as if we can have one without the other—and then we exorcise the direct presence of God out of our lives in the process. Yet we never seem to ask ourselves why we should not *experience* the Word of God itself, the Word saturated in His anointing Spirit—just as the ancient Hebrews did when the prophets were carried along by the Spirit, or as Paul indicated that the early Christians did when their faith stood not "in persuasive words of human wisdom" but "in *demonstration* of the Spirit and power" (1 Cor. 2:4). Jesus Himself declared that "the *words* I speak to you *are Spirit*" and that the kingdom of God would be "present in *power*" (John 6:63; Mark 9:1).

—On the Holy Spirit

The Importance of Frames

Often what seems to block a direct encounter with God is that people approach Him in the wrong mental frame to receive and participate in what God is saying in the way He is saying it. I use the word "frame" here to refer to any given worldview that becomes so embedded in people's thinking that they simply take its assumptions for granted without examining the foundations of their own thinking. Their frame of thought then becomes part of an unconscious way of perceiving and understanding reality. And, with virtually everyone, it is so habitual that it becomes, according to neurologists, encoded in the very functioning of their brains. So the frames within our brains become like labyrinths or mazes that only allow those thoughts to pass through that will follow the course which the labyrinth or maze lays out.

Such a course, however, can only end in personal disaster for a faith that "comes by hearing and hearing by the Word of God" (Rom. 10:17). Such a maze in our thinking, in other words, is calamitous to faith because, as one influential cognitive scientist says: "Frames are mental structures that *shape* the way we see the world. As a result, they *shape* the goals we seek," they *shape* "the plans we make," they *shape* "the way we act, and what counts as . . . good or bad" in the "outcome" of all of "our actions." So "in politics our frames shape our social policies."[29]

Even in the everyday life of a community, frames still shape our vision of what a community should be "and the institutions" that "we form" to ensure that those configurations maintain. Therefore, "to change our frames is to change all of this. Reframing *is* social change."[30] Reframing is also individual change. Reframing is cultural change. Reframing is total change.

Perhaps even more significantly, this linguist goes on to say: "You can't see or hear" such "frames. They are part of what cognitive scientists call the 'cognitive *unconscious*'— structures in our brains that we cannot consciously access.... Reframing is changing the way" people see "the world. It is changing what counts as common sense." And perhaps most suggestively for the issue at hand, "because language activates frames, new language," he says, "is required for new frames."[31]

—Building Christian Character

Rom. 12:1-2

New Frame, New Language

And they were all filled with the Holy Spirit and began to speak with other tongues, as the Spirit was giving them utterance.

—Acts 2:4

Here is a real key for learning to hear and participate in the life-changing words that someone speaks to us, especially when that someone is God. If we have the wrong frame, we simply won't hear, understand or experience God in the way He intended. Part of a genuine rebirth would, then, involve a complete change in frames.

But when a linguistics professor says that "a new language is required for a new frame," that in itself might well seem sufficient incentive for us to try to reframe everything about glossolalia and then to reexamine it in a more authentic context. And in such a new context, it can seem very plausible that in order for an alternative reality from God to emerge, for an alternative to the kingdoms of this world to come into being, a new and *unique language*—as is repeatedly described in the book of Acts, which also describes the birth of the church—would mark the birth of the Spirit into that new kingdom, into that entirely new "frame" of existence that Jesus said we must be reborn into. This new "frame" would put both the Biblical description and the current experience of glossolalia into a new context.

—*Building Christian Character*

Acts 2:1-18; 10:44-46; 11:15-18; 19:1-7; John 3:3, 5-8

The Firstborn of Many Brethren

Jesus, though He was the only begotten of the Father, was nonetheless also described as only "the *first*born of many brothers," the firstborn of many who would be brought to birth by the Spirit—He was not, in short, the "*last* born" (Rom. 8:29). We know this is true simply because God has now wondrously also "sent the *Spirit* of His Son into our hearts whereby we cry, 'Abba, Father.'" So we, too, have "received the Spirit of sonship" (Gal. 4:5; Rom. 8:15)—the same Spirit of absolute life that gave birth to Jesus and made Him the Son of God, as Peter proclaimed, has now astoundingly given rebirth to us as sons of God.

This powerful spiritual rebirth, then, is our first step onto the rock upon which Jesus said the church that hell would not prevail against would stand—this is the phenomenal initiation into a new and completely different order of life, an order of indestructible life that comes into being and grows to maturity only by the Spirit of God and within sons fathered by that power of life in its absolute form. The Spirit of life itself comes and enters human flesh and then increasingly leads that fleshly house into "all truth," building upon our initial experience with God until it ultimately brings us into conformity to the image of God's firstborn Son. This is what sets the scene for the astonishing drama between death and life in their absolute forms.

—All or Nothing?

John 16:7-13; Rom. 8:29

Empowerment as Sons

Hebrews 1:3-4 says that Christ, the Son, "sat down at the right hand . . . by becoming superior to the angels by inheriting a more excellent or superior name" (Heb. 1:3-4, JBR). The name and the source of His inheritance were tied together as one. And He has become "the firstborn of many brethren" in order that we, as members of His Body, might participate in His sonship by taking on His name and receiving the Spirit of sonship that comes under the guiding hand of the Father.

The Father wants us as His sons, wants us to sit at His right hand, so we can be empowered to build a culture of life on earth. The Father's right hand is the place of inheritance of the authority of God, the blessings of God, the place of preference, the place of grace, the place of redemption, the place of divine empowerment to bring the kingdom on earth as it is in heaven.

—*The Right Hand of Power*

Imagine that all around you is a secret place, a holy country, an unknown kingdom, an Israel not of land and sea but emerging straight out of the heart of God, a country not defined by earthly borders but coming down from heaven to invade and join together human hearts across the globe. Such a kingdom has no *physical* gateway to walk through. Yet a simple and direct means of access still lies open. Since it is a realm of spirit, the entranceway is a spiritual experience.

—*How Do You Know?*

Rom. 8:14-17; Gal. 4:1-9; Eph. 3:14-15; 1:20 with 2:6

Revealed unto Babes

Behold what manner of love the Father has bestowed on us, that we should be called children of God! Therefore the world does not know us, because it did not know Him.

—1 John 3:1

A dream is really a hope, but you cannot hope unless you trust, and you cannot trust unless you believe, and you cannot believe unless there is someone to believe in, and you cannot believe in someone unless you love them and unless you know they love you. So we dream because we love, and we love because we are loved—because we are the children of our Father, children who not only have known no better but have *chosen* to know nothing else.

I thank You, God, that when I myself must speak to others as a brother, as a husband, as a father, I may still in the secret places of my heart speak to You as Your child. "I thank You, Father, that You have hidden these things from the wise and the prudent and revealed them unto babes" (Matt. 11:25). So said the Lord Jesus.

—My Father's Child

A Promise for Believers

At the point where the Old Covenant closed and the New was on its way, Jesus instructed His disciples, "Behold, I send the Promise of My Father upon you; but tarry in the city of Jerusalem until you are endued with power from on high." He doesn't say, "Tarry until you believe." They were already believers, but this only prepared them for what was to come to them through their faith and the birth of the New Testament church. So He said to tarry until they received *power*. Scripture then says that at Pentecost, at *the very birth of the church* for those who were already believers in Christ, "all of [the disciples] were filled with the Holy Spirit and began to *speak* in *other tongues* as the *Spirit* enabled them" (Acts 2:4).

With such an important event, one so central to every aspect of salvation and the kingdom, those who see God as a God of love and consistency cannot accept that He would leave them with nothing as a compass needle to point to whether they have received the fullest possible experience of the Holy Spirit.

—*How Do You Know?*

The Promise Poured Out

And hope does not disappoint, because the love of God has been poured out within our hearts through the Holy Spirit who was given to us.

—*Romans 5:5*

On the Jewish holiday of Shavuot, the day of Pentecost, on the fiftieth day after the resurrection of the Hebrew Messiah, the gift of God's Holy Spirit was "poured out" on men and women. When immersed in these spiritual waters, the first followers of Jesus were swept into the streets of Jerusalem, shouting their praises of God, speaking in unknown languages, proclaiming His goodness and mercy and the great joy experienced by being overwhelmed in this Spirit.

Although it has been counterfeited and falsified, cheapened and degraded by the poor soil it has often coursed through, millions throughout the world have now once again enjoyed this wondrous gift, this great outpouring of God's Spirit. They are raising pure hands to the heavens in praise of their Creator as words in unknown languages spring forth in genuine supernatural power from the depths of their souls. As they speak those unknown words, they are taking the first steps into that new dimension of heavenly peace and joy, a dimension that surrounds each and every one of us. Their hearts are cleansed of doubt, lust, fear and depression. Their minds are made new by an ongoing faith in the supernatural love of the Holy One.

—*Experiencing God*

Living by the Power of God

Still others had trial of mockings and scourgings, yes, and of chains and imprisonment. They were stoned, they were sawn in two, they were tempted, they were slain with the sword. They wandered about in sheepskins and goatskins, being destitute, afflicted, tormented—of whom the world was not worthy. They wandered in deserts and mountains, in dens and caves of the earth. And all these, having obtained a good testimony through faith, did not receive the promise, God having provided something better for us, that they should not be made perfect apart from us.

—*Hebrews 11:36-40*

We are the ones upon whom the end of the age has come, the ones destined to receive the promise of the resurrection Spirit, the promise that reconstitutes us as sons of God and then leads us on in triumphal procession into "the full measure of the stature of Christ, a perfect man." Yes, this is the promise that carries us into the child of the promise, who *is* Christ—born of God.

Everything that has come to us has struggled its way down the long path of faith, a faith always reaching toward that day when the promised Holy Spirit would be poured out upon and fulfilled in the people of God. Theirs was not, then, a "partial faith" of some punctiliar moment of justification, a false faith, but a "whole faith," a great faith, a saving faith that is now attaining to what was promised and thus is "living . . . by the power of God."

—*False Faith versus Saving Faith*

Part XII
Fitly Framed Together

Laying Down Our Works

The root word of *charisma* is *charis*, or "grace," which means "gift." When anything's done by grace, it's a gift, a given. This means that a great deal of our prayer and efforts in so many areas of human existence, more than anything else, often in the end become little more than simply part of the struggle to lay down our own works. So at last they become only our "labor to enter into His rest." Only then can we come to view life as something received rather than as something we grasp for and take and fight to preserve as part of our own works and image.

—Givens and Losses

In the New Testament, the Greek word translated "unthankful" is *acharistos*, which literally means to be "without grace"; a person without gratitude is without grace.

—Building Christian Character

Clearing the Obscuring Rubble

Where you stand may be on an utterly twisted and debris-strewn path, one that you've thus far taken in order to achieve your own goals. If so, you must excavate through all the debris that you've heaped up on what God had originally planned for your life to bear witness to. Then, you must find out what His calling is for your life, what this gift is that you truly are to become. You can only do this through a long and deep outpouring of yourself in travailing prayer.

I think more than half the human labor that truly brings us to life amounts to merely clearing away debris we ourselves have heaped up on top of that life. Eliminating the garbage in our lives reduces and simplifies us enough that we can begin to hear God, that we can cease from our own labors and discover, in our newfound simplicity, just who we are to be in God.

—Givens and Losses

Laboring to Enter God's Rest

> *Let us therefore be diligent to enter that rest, lest anyone fall according to the same example of disobedience.*
>
> —*Hebrews 4:11*

We do "labor to enter into His rest," but this is like a mother laboring to be delivered of a child—it's something that comes upon us not by our choice but by the providential workings of everything involved to bring us to this place of labor and delivery. That kind of labor almost always, however, ends with our certainty that life, whether ours or that which we bring forth, is the gift of God.

It's not, in short, something we've conjured up in our hearts and minds, something we've brought to pass through our hard work, or something we think we're *supposed* to be doing as some sort of principled obligation.

—*Givens and Losses*

Grace Working in Us

To avoid sterility requires scraping away everything until we are reduced to the essence of what God has called us to be in our lives. Then, when we labor, we know what's laboring in us—not selfish ambition, not lust, envy, greed or pride, not covetousness, but only grace.

We may indeed labor more intensely than ever, but the supernatural nature of this energizing power, that it brings to birth through us things never possible to us before, makes us know that the energy is God working in us. So Paul declared, "By the grace of God, I am what I am, and . . . I worked harder than all of them. Yet it was not I but God who was working through me by His grace." Every believer should feel such certainty in such a gift.

—*Givens and Losses*

Leaving the Realm of Abstractions

No one can find their place in the Body by mere abstract thought or speculation but only by active and concrete participation in a specific place of service and relationship at a specific time with a specific people. They will, in short, begin to meet a real need that the Spirit specifically leads them to meet and then follow the unfolding path of service from there.

—Servants of Love

When a selfless and caring attitude prevails, when Jesus' love truly and fully motivates people, this releases everyone to not only want to do their best but also to actually begin to do it, since they will be filled with joy in the experience, joy in the powerful presence of the God who *is* love as He works in and through them by His resonant Spirit.

—What Kind of Family?

Tangible Love-Service

Love is the essence of Christianity, and the essence of love is giving.

—*Servants of Love*

Ultimately, to pour ourselves out in a tangible relationship of love-service will involve us in some way with every person whose life touches ours in the Body, and even in the world. And this is true whether in regard to the family (the husband, wife and children), the larger fellowship itself (submission to its divine order), our job (employer and employee) or any other sphere in our lives. Only by becoming what God has created us to be, by serving in the functions that He has made us to fill, can we pour out our tangible, real love to God. That is the only way that we can serve Him, the only tangible and real way we can submit to Him as our Lord. John said that we must love those we can see before we can claim to love Him whom we cannot see.

—*Servants of Love*

Acts 20:35; 1 John 3:16-18; 4:20

Becoming Transparent Vessels

We must see beyond the person whom we serve— we must see Jesus. We must see that we serve the Head when we serve the Body, and that the whole Body is all connected in an ascending order unto the Head, a great love-chain of service, and that we can only grow to maturity by finding our place in that great chain of being flowing from God.

Many believe that they have a great call on their lives. Yet no matter how great the call, our "gift will make room for us" only as we come into a *tangible and abiding* relationship of service to God's people, and only as we willingly become what God made us to be, no matter how great or small we may think our calling is. What proves of utmost importance is that the heart of service that motivated Jesus Himself should also motivate us, that we desire only to serve Him in the way He has made us to serve.

If we are truly sensitive to the needs of our brothers and sisters, that is, if we are motivated by our love for them because we have bound ourselves as love-slaves to them, then we will anticipate their needs. And when we have served them, they will hardly even be aware of our presence or service, for what they will feel is the presence of the Lord and His burden and ministry and love for them. This leaves little room for the vainglory of the flesh.

—Servants of Love

John 12:21; 15:1-10; 2 Cor. 5:16; 1 Cor. 12:4-14, 18, 27-28; Prov. 18:16

"Each Part Does Its Share"

That we . . . may grow up in all things into Him who is the head—Christ—from whom the whole body, joined and knit together by what every joint supplies, according to the effective working by which every part does its share, causes growth of the body for the edifying of itself in love.

—Ephesians 4:14-16

The Body of Christ, as Paul insisted, is not made up of all equal parts in the sense that they are the same and are to be treated exactly the same. If so, then how could Paul command: "Let the elders who rule well be counted worthy of *double* honor, especially those who labor in the word and doctrine" (1 Tim. 5:17-18)? The people of God are not interchangeable parts of machinery—we are distinctly different members of the Body.

Only when "each part does its work" can the wisdom and glory of God be fully manifested. Each member, impelled by the burden of agape love, motivated by the desire to be what Jesus Christ has made him to be, must function in his place in the Body.

—Servants of Love

1 Cor. 12:15-19, 29-31

Growing to a Place of Maturity

When we, both individually and corporately, become the servant that God has ordained us to be, then we shall truly find that place of maturity from which we can fully reflect the glory of Jesus Christ to a dissolute world.

Then we shall no longer do anything "out of selfish ambition or vain conceit," but our motive shall be the love of Jesus. Of us it will be said that our attitude has become "the same as that of Christ Jesus: Who, being in very nature God, did not consider equality with God something to be grasped, but *made Himself nothing*, taking the very *nature of a servant*, being made in human likeness. And being found in appearance as a man, He *humbled Himself* and became *obedient to death*—even death on a cross!" (Phil. 2:5-8).

We shall then approach the goal of perfecting our temples, sharing in His sufferings and rejoicing that He has counted us worthy to do so. God will then add to us those remaining members of His holy house as He fills up that great corporate temple for which Jesus will someday return. As that day approaches, God will use a faceless people who have made themselves truly His servants by letting the face of God shine through them. They shall serve God Himself to this world. They shall manifest His supernatural power to comfort, to pour forth His holy love, to turn the hearts of the fathers to the children and the children to the fathers, to gather His children into the garner, before He burns the chaff with unquenchable fire.

—Servants of Love

Meaning Found in Relationship

If meaning comes from the relation any given elements have to one another, then a door hung in space is meaningless in that it is totally unrelated to its surroundings. And, in fact, I once hung a door from the rafters to see what people coming to a particular meeting would think of it. They were all reluctant to still call something so totally wrenched from the context that gave it meaning a "door."

Such a "door" serves as neither an entrance nor an exit. But if we took the same "door," which in that circumstance seemed so absurd or alarming, and put it in its proper place, in its appropriate setting of *relationships*, then we would simply take its meaning for granted. We wouldn't even think about things such as "meaning." *Design*, in the sense of how things are related, becomes almost everything in regard to finding *meaning* and working out relationships. Thus Paul tells us that "God has *composed* the Body" "just as He wanted it to be" (1 Cor. 12:18, 24).

Many, of course, say that they want relationship, not form; but form *is* relationship, and without form, there is no relationship—only confusion and chaos, and conflict and turmoil, all marked by not only unjoined pieces but also unjoined lives.

—What Kind of Family?

Suddenly Reoriented

We see in part. We know in part. But God sees all things, and He knows exactly where you need to be. And that knowledge and understanding creates in you the humility that "comes before honor." Suddenly you see yourself and what your true limitations really are, and it humbles you.

Just go out in the woods sometime. This only happened to me once. But it provided a more than sufficient awakening. I was wandering in a wilderness area that was relatively flat with no visible landmarks, but very densely forested. It was overcast. You couldn't tell exactly where the sun was, and toward the afternoon I said, "Hmmm, it's getting late. I better head in. Which direction is in?" If you experience that sort of thing one time in your life, then you'll know the vertiginous, almost panicky feeling that comes with being lost. You'll know what it feels like to have limitations.

It happens to some of you all the time spiritually, and yet you don't know it because someone's always there with a raised eyebrow, a frown, a gentle hand of restraint on the arm or shoulder. And we respond, "Oh, Dad's right there. I was getting out of orbit a little." Suddenly, the whole world is reoriented, and you know your place. And you should feel relieved, not stifled by or resentful toward those who have oriented you.

—Coming into Orbit

"Complete in Him"

I do not pray for these alone, but also for those who will believe in Me through their word; that they all may be one, as You, Father, are in Me, and I in You; that they also may be one in Us, that the world may believe that You sent Me.

—John 17:20-21

Ultimately, recognizing one's own limitations means at least one thing: God will not reveal to *each* of us *directly everything* that we need to know to walk with God into the fullness of salvation.

—Acknowledging God's Word

Believers are not to merely discern the extent and magnitude of our own gifts and functions or their importance to the Body. Rather, we must also discern the limits of our gifts, functions and importance to the Body and see how much more important to us are the gifts of others, and especially the whole. In short, if we are to attain unity, we must walk in deep humility of mind, "esteeming others better than ourselves." We must decrease in our individual self-importance so that Christ may increase in the wholeness of His corporate witness.

—Communion and Discerning of the Body

There are so many things in life that leave me bewildered. I have stood awed and puzzled more than once, and then someone will come to me—often my wife, my children, a brother, it doesn't matter who—and they'll tell me simple

---

1 Cor. 12:3, 5, 11, 17-21, 28; Eph. 4:10-16; 1 Pet. 4:10; 5:5; Heb. 13:7, 17; Phil. 2:3-8; Acts 20:19, 35; Rom. 12:3; James 4:6-10

words that suddenly seem to give such plain and clear direction, scarcely even knowing what they're giving to me. But, everything falls into place for me. Afterwards, I wonder how I could have been so blind, so ignorant. But it's because God intended that there should be many areas of our lives not covered by our own gifts. We need our brothers and sisters, just as Paul insisted that we do.

—*Givens and Losses*

Any person disconnected from the Body of Christ—anyone who cannot point to direct, ongoing and abiding relationships with Spirit-filled Christians, relationships that connect each member to a specific place in that Body joined in submission to the Head, to God's authority—has failed in the most basic requirement of living for God: the humility that breaks life-destroying pride.

—*Bedrock*

1 Cor. 12:12-28

Commissioned to Go Forth

God did not intend for one human life to abide alone. Like a grain of wheat, Jesus died, and multitudes have since risen from His death. Jesus is the Head of the stalk, but believers are the full grain in the Head.

He is the true vine, but believers are the branches. Just as the physical hand of Jesus became the true extension of God's right hand of spiritual power in human flesh, and just as He was given all power in heaven and on earth, so, too, He has now commissioned His people to go forth as the means through which the right hand of God's spiritual power shall extend and manifest itself in human flesh to the ends of the earth.

—*Right Hand of Power*

John 12:24; 15:1-8; Mark 4:27-29; Matt. 28:19; Acts 1:8

God's Manifold Wisdom

This is the "eternal" purpose for which God has called the church: "His intent was that *now, through the church, the manifold wisdom of God should be made known* to the rulers and authorities in the heavenly realms, according to His *eternal purpose* which He accomplished in Christ Jesus our Lord" (Eph. 3:10-11). Through the church, then, God desires to declare His glory, to express His wisdom, to all the heavens and the earth.

This "manifold wisdom" of God is a comprehensive wisdom that encompasses every area of life. The word translated in Ephesians 3:10 as "manifold" is in the Greek polupoikilos, "a strengthened form of poikilos, 'most varied.'"[32] By using the form polupoikilos in speaking of the "manifold wisdom" of God, the Scriptures emphasize that "the wisdom of God has shown itself in Christ to be varied beyond measure and in a way which surpasses all previous knowledge thereof."[33]

This wisdom encompasses more, takes on more diverse and various forms, than anyone has ever before imagined. It includes all "things in heaven and things on earth" (Eph. 1:10) that minister life and strength: "Every good and perfect gift is from above, coming down from the Father of the heavenly lights" (James 1:17).

God meets every need of the spirit, soul and body through the *charismata*, the "gifts," that He distributes to and through His people. He has given His people gifts and skills and crafts to meet every natural or practical need, as well as every spiritual need.

—Wisdom's Children, Book Two

"Wisdom Builds Her House"

Wisdom is the ability to perceive relationships, the whole interlinked series and patterns of relationships within which any individual person, thing or act can truly live. This self-evidently requires a view of reality transcendent to merely human viewpoints.

Wisdom enables us to perceive the form, the pattern of relationships, in which any individual act takes place, to recognize the fullness of all the interrelationships between that individual act and the wide diversity of its effects and ramifications. Wisdom, then, gives us the ability to bring something forth in wholeness, completeness, the ability to see the proper form in which something must exist in order to develop into the fullness that God intended. Wisdom is, in short, she who builds her house; for what is a house but a series of relationships of various shapes and forms that together can hold the content of life?

—Wisdom's Children, Book Two

Prov. 9:1

Building a Dwelling Place for God

We now know our goal: to build a new temple of our lives, a temple for God's spirit to inhabit.

—Taking the First Step

Do you not know that you are the temple of God and that the Spirit of God dwells in you?

—1 Corinthians 3:16

Thus Rabbi Ibn Ezra said, "Man is a microcosm," and Rabbi Yose the Galilean also wrote, "Whatever the Holy One . . . created in His world, He created in man."[34] Centuries later, influential twentieth-century scholars were still similarly describing each human being as a "miniature local Universe containing all the principles of total Universe."[35]

This is a notion that appears and reappears throughout history, for instance, in Shakespeare: "What a piece of work is a man, how noble in reason, how infinite in faculties, in form and moving, how express and admirable in action, how like an angel in apprehension, how like a god: the beauty of the world; the paragon of animals."[36] Or similarly, the twentieth-century "Renaissance Man," R. Buckminster Fuller, once described each human being as a "miniature local Universe containing all the principles of total Universe."[37]

Jesus would encapsulate the same sense of human worth and magnitude when He declared that one soul was worth the whole world, and Moses, Jeremiah and Paul would all teach variations on the same theme of the human being as "the temple of the living God; as God has said, I will

---

Matt. 16:26

dwell in them, and walk in them; and I will be their God, and they shall be My people" (Lev. 26:12; Jer. 32:38; Ezek. 37:27; 2 Cor. 6:16, KJV).

Finally, when the Psalmist exclaimed, "I am fearfully and wonderfully made" (Ps. 139:14, NIV), he was expressing insight into the same notion: that man was to be the supreme immanent expression on earth of the transcendent God's very present image: a physical being virtually at-one in and with God's love and truth, God's peace and joy.

—*A Garden Enclosed*

Perfectly Coordinated

The place into which God has arranged for us to fit is our place in His Body. God has ordained a definite and living form for this Body, a form through which each of us is tied to every other person through each one's place in God. That form entails the submission of the parts to one another according to the living pattern of God, just as the parts of the physical body must submit to one another in order for the biological organism as a whole to work effectively. To the extent that the members fail to do this, the body becomes spastic: limbs fly out randomly, helter-skelter and in conflict with one another. Likewise, only when each part of the spiritual Body submits perfectly in its place can this spiritual organism function as the unified, perfectly coordinated expression of the God perfectly at one with Himself.

—Wisdom's Children, Book Two

To acknowledge the truth can only mean to find our place in the Christ who *is* the truth. This, in turn, can only mean to find our place in His corporate Body; for there is no direct joining to Christ, to the Head, apart from the God-given, "fitly framed" order of His Body.

—Acknowledging God's Word

John 14:6; Eph. 2:20-22; 4:15-16; 1 Cor. 12:12-13; Ezek. 37:1-14

Part XIII
"Radical Possibilities"

"Progress" or Simplicity?

They think it strange that you do not run with them in the same flood of dissipation.

—1 Peter 4:4

The world we live in makes of our minds a cultural carousel where we are always spinning in circles, grasping for the shiny ring of the new, the latest, the most recent. Soon the carousel seems merely like an ever-faster-moving conveyor belt of "progress" on which we're trapped, one speeding on so rapidly that we're too frightened to leap from it. But before long, we usually develop a growing anxiety that the carousel has turned into a spiral, and then the spiral has turned into a descending conveyor belt headed ever faster toward nothing but the great Gehenna dump of death.

As for our own community, something of real substance underlies our return to the simplicity that once marked the wholeness of human culture. If we let ourselves be drawn out of that simplicity and into the always new, we are going to lose the very essence and vision of who and what we are—the essence and vision of wholeness, which is the vision of life, even eternal life, a life that God is *still* offering to people.

—*Aporia and the Collapse of Cultures*

Bedrock Alone

So Jesus said, "Therefore everyone who hears these words of Mine and puts them into practice is like a wise man who built his house on the rock. The rain came down, the floods rose, the winds blew and beat against that house; yet it did not fall, because it had its foundation on the rock. But everyone who hears these words of Mine and does not put them into practice is like a foolish man who built his house on sand. The rain came down, the floods rose, and the winds blew and beat against that house, and great was its fall."

—Matthew 7:24-27

The house of custom and tradition can only stand the test of time if it is built upon something more enduring than the windblown dunes of changing epochs with all their shifting shapes and forms, their drifting trends and fashions, all of which blow hither and thither with no rhyme or meaning. Foundations of sand always erode under the force of the winds, rains and floods, under the force of everything that brings the inevitable daily vicissitudes of human existence. Only bedrock remains immovable in the storm.

And how many houses built on sand have recent generations seen collapse under such turbulent changes in the social or cultural climate? The house of mindless faith in human progress fell in the muddy trenches of Flanders, sunk in the muck and mud of a million casualties in the single battle of the Somme.

The hope-filled house of technology and science as the panacea for all human problems, needs and longings began to slide into the grave at the burial pits of Auschwitz and Hiroshima, not to mention the part technology has played in a galloping pollution and in the depletion of the earth's environment. The house of human rationalism infell with the black holes deduced from Einstein's theory of general relativity and with quantum indeterminacy. Other political, social, economic and intellectual houses have met a similar demise, along with many of our much more personal houses.

—*Leaving the Lonely Labyrinth*

Aporia: Catalyst for Radical Change

German philosopher Martin Heidegger used the word aporia to refer to a state of mind totally paralyzed by pervasive doubt. It is a mind-set of doubt so severe, so broad, so deep, so all-encompassing, that people lose their ability to constructively think or act.[38] They freeze up, at a total loss as to how they might even approach what has become a flood of cascading problems that has no visible limits in volume, expanse and depth. The irresistible, chaotic and overwhelming force simply sweeps them along, and they begin to drown in waves of crisis after crisis.

No one has any idea what course should be followed, what direction should be taken, either to escape or to overcome the upheaval all around and within them, so they become immobilized. This is true even when it feels like everything around them is spiraling into an "abyss" of "chaos."[39]

It even becomes impossible to distract oneself with diversions or entertainments because the crisis has reached such proportions and has become so threatening that the individual feels he must do *something*, even though he can think of nothing to do.

At this point, people either lose their emotional and mental equilibrium or come to a complete reframing of their entire lives and worldview. There are times in history where the crises, the questions and the doubts take on epochal proportions—in short, they pervade the whole culture. Thus, Václav Havel, former president of the Czech Republic and considered one of the four most influential intellectuals of the twentieth century, spoke of great periods of transition "when it seems that something is on the way out and something else is painfully being born. It is as if something were crumbling, decaying, and exhausting itself, while something else, still indistinct, were arising from the rubble."[40]

He goes on to say that "periods of history when values undergo a fundamental shift are certainly not unprecedented."[41] People during these times even begin to question the nature of their own being and what they are doing, their own essence and existence.[42] So Havel says that today, modern "man as an observer is becoming completely alienated from himself as a being"[43]—he only experiences himself as another object swept along in the technological cornucopia of modernity.

—Aporia and the Collapse of Cultures

Flying or Falling?

The kind of transformation that can bring a radically different reality, culture and way of life only happens, at least on a mass scale, when some major cultural crisis causes people to question, on the deepest levels, the prevailing ways in which they have been looking at the world. Such times have happened at great turning points of history, and many trends in the world's cultures, polities and economies indicate that we may now again be heading toward such a time.

At such moments, people recognize the necessity of changing course. But when we begin to change course, we must break completely free of the old framework, the old paradigms, or our course can only end once again in failure, if not disaster.

No community can pretend to be "flying" as a truly sustainable community when it is knowingly still violating the "principles of aerodynamics," the principles of a self-sustaining life. Unless we change frames completely, we're going to crash, no matter how much we pretend that we are flying. We must, in short, make the shift to another model if we're truly going to fly—to a different cultural paradigm, to a new frame, a new frontier.

—The Political-Economic Primer

Radical Possibilities

When epoch-changing times descend upon any people, they demand answers to desperate questions about matters it never even occurred to people to ask before. And when they finally do, it often then opens their minds for the first time to the possibilities of radically different ways of thinking, acting and living that they formerly never gave a thought to.

These differences then begin to take on form and definition, shaping up to become a vision of a dramatically altered world, a world that most never imagined they could even seriously consider or picture, much less inhabit. Eventually, however, more and more people begin to long for such an alternative world, a new order of relationships—whether with people, creation or God—until the longing builds to critical mass.

—Life Against Death

Preparing to Offer Hope

What we call human culture, human society, American society, is in many ways as fragile as a haphazardly built house of stacked business cards. Anything could bring it down, as was shown by the magnitude of the shakings caused by the terrorist bombing of the World Trade towers or even by the natural disaster of Hurricane Katrina. But the great cultural earthquake and shaking that so many see as threatening us today would surely bury such a fragile infrastructure and its culture.

So before that comes, I hope the warning tremors will begin to dislodge people, and especially, perhaps, Christians, at least those among the remnant that do not worship at mammon's altar, that have not bowed a knee to Baal. I hope the aporia, the all-encompassing doubt about the life they're living, about the intricate but empty theologies they cling to, will begin to rearrange their thinking and open them to the possibility of answers they've refused to even consider before. I feel a profound need that we should press on in our individual lives, in our family life and in our corporate, collective life to bring to as much fulfillment and completion as possible the vision and reality of what people will need to see and hear in order to believe they can gain escape velocity from all this.

We also must have at hand written blueprints for such a life so that people can quickly erect the structure for such communities—just as the early Jewish settlements in 1937-39 were built by people moving into an area early in the morning, before dawn, with all the ready-made constituent pieces for a kibbutz—walls, towers and essential buildings. Then, in one day, a hundred people would assemble those pieces into a Jewish settlement and be living there by the time the sun set and their enemies, who fought only at night, attacked them.

Only in our case, the "ready-made" constituent elements must include not only the material elements but, much more importantly, the spiritual. So what then does God want us to be and do in the days that are coming? And what if those days are much closer than we think they are?

—Aporia and the Collapse of Cultures

Part XIV
"A City Set on a Hill"

Called Out

> *"Come out from among them and be separate," says the Lord. "Do not touch what is unclean, and I will receive you. I will be a Father to you, and you shall be My sons and daughters."*
>
> —2 Corinthians 6:17-18

The church was not called upon to intrude into the order of the kingdoms of the world to force its own vision on a fallen culture, but to become the church, the *ekklesia*, the "called out" Body of reconstituted people who stood separately as a counterposing kingdom and culture "not of this world," a "city set upon a hill," one that was "complete in" Christ, therefore one having its own unique kind of education, vocations, lifestyle, community relationships and so on. Every area of the life of the individual—culture, education, vocation, birth, death, aging, the provision of food, shelter and clothing, the order of human relationships—was to be brought out of the world and into the kingdom of God, into the church.

—*Education Exodus*

Authentic Unity

Our great motive over the decades can perhaps best be summed up as a desire to participate in the creation of what one man has called "communities of exemplary Christian existence."[44]

Such communities would have several purposes, all amplifying and expressing the most commonly assumed soteriological ones. One of these purposes would simply be, as one theologian has stated, to "teach us how to live authentically" in the presence of God and other people.[45] Such communities would also hopefully make wise choices possible in religion, culture, relationships, vocations and lifestyle, and "on a scale large enough to make a difference."[46] They would be communities where children, women and men share the ineffable delight of experientially knowing God, communities where word and deed are fused in the authentic unity of a lived life.

—*What We Believe*

A "Spiritual Convenience Store"?

The kingdom of heaven is like a merchant seeking fine pearls, and upon finding one pearl of great value, he went and sold all that he had and bought it.

—Matthew 13:45-46

The church is not to be merely an emergency prayer station for spiritual refueling in times of crisis, situated alongside the fast lane of contemporary culture and serving as a sort of spiritual fast fuel and food adjunct, some pit stop or convenience store on our racecourse down that secular culture's linear expressway to the fulfillment of our personal ambitions. Nor do we love people just to pull them into our "Amen Corner," into our cheering or rooting section, so that we can easily manipulate and control them according to our own personal desires, goals and ambitions. Rather, the church is to serve as the new cultural context for a complex and multi-dimensional new life in God that is called "the kingdom."

—*Salvation as Exodus*

A Means for Healing

God's Word does not provide a pattern for meeting the extraordinary needs of contemporary social crises by herding millions of displaced persons in a shell-shocked, humanistic society into appropriate food lines, beds and so forth, dropping them onto the conveyor belt at one end and letting it dump them out wherever it may at the other.

Rather, it provides the means for the healing of the shell-shocked millions themselves, for the re-creation of men and women who will pass through the barbican of the kingdom to become responsible human beings before the God who rules in another world by love. The Bible offers the pattern through which the family and church, the living systems that, even in their most crippled and handicapped forms, many people have used down through the millennia to care for the needy and to rear the young, can be remade to work more effectively than ever for these purposes.

—*Why Build Agrarian Christian Communities?*

Self-Sufficient in Christ

Thy kingdom come, Thy will be done; on earth, as it is in heaven.

—Matthew 6:10

In the completeness and wholeness of Christ is self-sufficiency, not leaning upon what would make us partakers of a system run by something totally opposed to and at enmity with God. So the Scripture is *full* of admonition, warning, rebuke about everything that would tie us to such a world and to such a system. These admonitions are not peripheral to the Word of God. They are part and parcel of what Paul meant when he said, "You are complete" in Christ (Col. 2:10). So if our *whole* life is to be lived in Christ and we are "complete in Him," then our whole life should be self-sufficient in Christ—not dependent on the world or its systems and provisions.

—The Supernatural Power of Greed

---

2 Tim. 2:4; 1 Tim. 6:6-12; 1 John 2:15-17; James 4:1-5; 2 Cor. 6:14-18; Rev. 18:1-5

A Functioning Alternative

Where the therapeutic State has utterly failed, the church can succeed, if only she'll thoroughly disentangle herself from the embrace of such a culture. Again, the answer is not to let government do it all, but for government to step out of its role of pseudo-god and let the transcendent God transform families and churches, empowering them to fulfill their functions in training responsible and productive members of a new society—people who will be truly happy in being just what they were made to be. Such a functioning alternative in the Christian church today is only now, at most, a cloud the size of a man's fist. But with the growing crisis of secular society and the therapeutic State, more and more Christians are seeing that the church must become such a complete alternative. And it is not difficult to hear the sound of rain pouring down just over the crest of the next mountain. You can even sniff its fragrance in the dry desert air.

—*Why Build Agrarian Christian Communities?*

The Mountain of Inheritance

New Testament scriptures describe the heavenly Jerusalem as a mountain—Mount Zion—something that rises above all the surrounding terrain, a place of far-reaching vision, a place worth ascending to, a place to look up to in awe, a place that is higher than we are and that transcends us and our circumstances or ambitions. This is that "city . . . set on a hill [that] cannot be hidden" (Matt. 5:14).

It is the "mountain" of "inheritance," the inheritance of Yahweh's very identity as that identity is expressed in redeeming love's authority and power on earth, the place where children can be born to become the heirs of salvation. And Isaiah tells us, "Say unto Zion, 'Thou art My people'" (Isa. 51:16, KJV). So the Biblical view sees Zion, which is Yahweh's throne, as God's people. These are the people who have entered into the place of Yahweh's inheritance, which is the place of His name.

—Right Hand of Power

Heb. 12:22; Ps. 132:13-14

"In Your Midst"

For the kingdom of God is not eating and drinking, but righteousness and peace and joy in the Holy Spirit.

—Romans 14:17

A world of wonder, joy, peace, splendor, stands at the fingertips of all whose eyes God has opened to see. So near is it that it whispers its great promise to those attuned to the Holy Spirit's resounding call. I am speaking of the kingdom of God. It is not a physical dimension, but a spiritual realm, the dimension where God breathes directly into human lives, where a supernatural, redeeming love begins to rule us. Thus Paul explained, "He is not far from each one of us. 'For in Him we live and move and have our being'" (Acts 17:27). And Jesus said, "The kingdom of God is not coming with signs to be observed; nor will they say, 'Look, here it is!' or 'There it is!' For behold, the kingdom of God is in your midst" (Luke 17:20-21).

—*Experiencing God*

Making the Most of Every Opportunity

The spiritual kingdom of God is the only place into which He has consecrated His government, His laws, His justice, His dominion, His authority and His sovereignty—this Body of people that He is connecting to His own Headship and "has prepared to do His will." And this spiritual kingdom of God does not come forth in a vacuum. It has a competitor, and that competitor also presses forth daily to establish his opposing dominion. Paul admonishes, "Make the most of every opportunity, for the days are evil" (Eph. 5:15-16). The word for "evil" in this scripture means "to actively work against" all that is righteous.

We must make the most of every opportunity to serve God with all our hearts because the evil one actively seeks to oppose God's people (even unto death), and he does so at every opportunity. He continually "prowls around like a roaring lion, looking for someone to devour" (1 Pet. 5:8).

—Servants of Love

Ever-Clearer Contrast

The shining forth of natural light on anything of substance (like sunlight on the moon) automatically creates contrast to and separation from the natural surrounding darkness. So when God's light shines forth through the Word that is heaven's lamp and on people of substance, of integrity and character, it must bring forth greater spiritual separation from the surrounding world's darkness. As the greater light of the Word shines in the darkness, the contrast between light and darkness becomes clearer, and through this increasing contrast, the *form* onto which the light pours, the form of the covenant people of God, the Body of Christ, also becomes delineated with greater clarity against the backdrop of the surrounding world. As the "values" increase in their contrast, the form of the Body of Christ (like that of the moon) grows more visible, as does its detailed diversity—that is, its texture and "color."

—*Leaving the Lonely Labyrinth*

Ps. 119:105; Rom. 12:4-5

Culture of the Covenant

Love is the only force I know of powerful enough to bring people into a place of oneness with God. Whatever a person loves, he conforms himself to.

—*Total Repentance*

Captured in the egocentric *soil* of Babylon, in a spiritual geography and topography of hardpan selfishness, of unmitigated confusion and ignorance about roles, functions and sense of place, no one can sing the self-sacrificial *love songs* of Zion, of a "city united together as one" (Ps. 122:3). Lack of proper soil (and soil, as every farmer knows, has a tenaciously formal structure[47]) means failure to realize the covenant love for which everyone claims to long. Lack of proper soil leads to the inability to grow the fruit of love. Without the proper patterns of *structural relationship* among the members of the Body one to another, the full *love relationship* becomes all but impossible. Without the mature recognition by each of exactly what God has made him or her to be, the Body can never grow to maturity.

—*Leaving the Lonely Labyrinth*

Faithful to the Form

The Body is the anointed form through which God's life can flow through the ministries God has sent, just as sap moves through the trunk and limbs of the tree.
—*Acknowledging God's Word*

Believers will never find fulfillment without binding themselves in covenant to the *form* of a specific place, a time, a situation and a people—in other words, within the *form* of the Body of Christ. This is so because it's only the form that shall be filled with all the fullness of God, the church that is His fullness. And this church is made up of people who know what it means to stand by their word. The Lord of heaven stood by His Word some two millennia ago; and He still stands by His Word today. His Word was made flesh and dwelt among us, and He bore faithfully the burden to incarnate God's truth in the conduct of His life. He bore this faithfulness out, literally, even to "the edge of doom."

So His love was not "time's fool." He bore it out past the ravaging reach of time's stone-cold hand, past death, hell and the grave. His love emerged triumphant over time as He passed from the temporal into the eternal. He stood by His Word, and on Him a name is written, "Faithful and True." The form that He then fulfilled was the "form of a servant" (Phil. 2:7, KJV). And those who will be His people and bear His name will be a people who stand by their word, fulfilling the form that He filled full—the form of their love service within the larger form of Messiah's corporate Body.

These will not be a people who must be pumped up again

Eph. 1:23; Acts 2:23-27; Rev. 1:18

and again, a people seeking only the empty satisfactions of spiritual lusts, filling the perforated bag held in the hands of people living in a perforated culture that cannot possibly hold the content of God. Those merely seeking their own interests, like children in a sweet shop, will never know either the agony or the ecstasy of the cross and resurrection. But anyone who determines to know God in this way will soon find their place among a people possessing an "infinite passion," a people that express themselves in lives that stand by words, a people who are faithful to the form, to the covenant of the cross, filling it up and bringing its promise home.

—Love That Works

New Covenant Covering

The private chambers of both the corporate and individual temples formed by God's covenant provide the sanctuaries where a fallen, death-bound people can begin to have communion with God's everlasting life.

—*Love That Works*

The highest example of covenant is when a believer turns to God, when he willingly exposes his life to God in the hope that his sins will be covered in Christ, buried under the New Covenant of Jesus' blood, thus allowing the new believer to become one with Messiah and His Body. The believer can then look forward to an increasing oneness with God, and the individual's life can find meaning and purpose in Christ. To repeat, such an exposure of the innermost essence of an individual, of one's very being, demands the highest order of protection; for God made the human heart a temple to hold the greatest of all treasures, His Spirit, His love.

So Christians, as God's "treasured possession," as long as they remain in the world, must remain *hidden* in the field of the world, covered by God's New Covenant, by the corner of His robe, by the wings of His sanctuary.

The church has an integrity and a reality of life that extends beyond any individual member, a life only experienced as love flows *between* its members in that order of relationships designed by God. And only in this plexus of relationships can the true image of Christ emerge on earth—can Jesus continue to come in our human flesh.

—*Love That Works*

Col. 3:3; Mal. 3:17, NIV; Matt. 13:44; Ruth 2:12; 3:9; Ps. 17:8; 36:7; 57:1; 61:3-4; 63:7; 91:1-4, 9

So the law cannot bring forth the positive image that God has called people to because the image of Christ necessitates transcending the fallen human nature that continually and centrifugally spins out and down in a perennial spiral to chaos. The image of Christ can only be imparted by supernaturally imparting to people the very nature of God, which is transcendent love, the very Spirit of Christ. Law, by somewhat restraining evil acts, can only at best neutralize the actions of the fallen nature, that which opposes the manifestation of the image of Christ. Only the workings of God's grace, however, can impart the image and power of God to the soul.

—A Garden Enclosed

---

1 John 4:8, 16

The Experience of Covenant Love

When you love something enough to give your life to it, you want to make the means and the end one.

—*Givens and Losses*

"God is love," John declared (1 John 4:8, 16). And so we can only know Him by entering into the supernatural *experience* of covenant love. Concepts or forms of covenant are not enough: we must experience God as if He actually existed, if in fact He does actually exist. The form is only created in order to hold the content. The theological menu can only at best prepare us for the meal. This *experience* is the purpose for which Jesus Christ was sacrificed, so that man and God could come into actual communion—"union with" one another. The ongoing *experience* of covenant love is the powerful, the beautiful, the fulfilling realization of that communion. Everything else only prepares for an unfolding of that experiential relationship.

—*Leaving the Lonely Labyrinth*

A commitment to sacrificial love proves utterly impossible for lapsed human flesh. People must be thoroughly reoriented by a powerful infilling of God's Spirit that invades and transforms human experience. Then this spiritual grafting, severed from one tree and suffused with life from another world, must be immediately planted in a cultural tree that stands far taller, broader and more deeply rooted than what most churches today have even considered providing. Such a tree only grows in a culture that can sustain and develop this sort of supernatural experience. Apart from this, no meaningful covenant is possible. But with it, everything we long for and need lies before us.

—Why Build Agrarian Christian Communities?

Living in Harmony

> *True fulfillment comes only when we complete a purpose or meet a necessity that transcends ourselves. It is like learning to sing a new song: we don't simply do what we feel like; rather, the song already has its own form to which we must conform our voice, our heart, our soul.*
>
> —*Wisdom's Children*

There is something in us, in spite of our programming to the contrary, that wants to be validated as valuable human beings by *other* human beings, even though (or even especially when) those others must necessarily in some measure differ from us—there is, in short, something about harmony and symphony that strikes us somehow as grander than merely singing alone or even in unison, and this is simply because a symphony takes instruments, sounds and voices that differ from one another and yet still makes them somehow come together in something unified, beautiful, powerful and whole. So in this sense, loving yourself can never compete with loving and being loved by another.

—*What's the Problem with Love?*

Progressing in Unity

It is an absolute necessity to preserve "the unity of the Spirit in the bond of peace" as God brings us to that place of "unity in the faith." But at some point something must happen that takes us across a line and into the realization of the unity that will bring us into "the full measure of the stature of Christ, a perfect man" (Eph. 4:13). When we cross this line into the territory that carries us toward "the unity of the faith," when we know that God is leading us and guiding us by His Spirit "into *all* truth"—only then is it confirmed that our claim to be preserving "the unity of the Spirit" was not a sham, a hollow claim that was taking us nowhere but into the world's stagnant definition of a dubious tolerance that destroys truth and, in the name of pluralism, implements a coerced polytheism that denies the liberty to worship the God who is One.

If what we call the "unity of the Spirit" is stagnant, is not moving toward the goal of the unity of the faith, then we are *not* following the Spirit that "leads and guides into all truth." And our unity of the spirit may be the unity only of the world's spirit, the *zeitgeist*, but it is not the unity of *God's* Spirit. For His Spirit is not stationary. It's a living, moving force of life that takes us toward, and then ever more deeply into, the one true God and His great purpose on earth—"this is eternal life, . . . that they may know . . . the only true God, and Jesus Christ whom [He has] sent" (John 17:3). So God's Spirit, because it's taking us into the life of Christ's Body, is also taking us into wholeness, into God's oneness and unity on every level, into God's eternal life. This isn't a unity based on human tolerance or on any other self-righteous human notions or works. This is a unity only God can bring about through people who have totally surrendered their own ideas to

Him, a people who can truthfully say to this God, "We utterly belong to You."

—*So You Want Community?*

We must truly belong to one another, not merely in some "theoretical," "mystical" sense, but by actually and authentically participating in one another's lives, sharing in each other's gifts, services, experiences, sorrows, joys, victories, burdens and activities.

—*Wisdom's Children, Book One*

---

1 Cor. 12:26

A Call to Repentance

Ridicule comes on the church as a whole when the world looks upon the unfinished work of the church's restoration to its original spiritual power, devotion and order. "Where," the world asks, "is the love, the power, the miracles, the unity, the life so vividly recounted in the book of Acts? Why is the church today not like that depicted in the Bible? If the first church was so 'primitive' and this one today so progressive, why hasn't it exceeded the first in power, in love, in unity, in miracles, in turning 'the world upside down'?"

—*Total Repentance*

If we are truly burdened to see the church become that which God said that it should be in the last days, when the glory of the latter house shall exceed the glory of the former, if we honestly desire to see the world come to believe that Jesus manifests God, then we must fall on our faces before the Lord and cry out to Him in absolute brokenness until the divisions that separate us are also broken down completely.

—*Forming Christ's Body, Book One*

Hag. 2:9

A Call to Restoration

Repent therefore and be converted, that your sins may be blotted out, so that times of refreshing may come from the presence of the Lord, and that He may send Jesus Christ, who was preached to you before, whom heaven must receive until the times of restoration of all things.

—Acts 3:19-21

In these times, Yahweh once again is building up, restoring, His spiritual nation, His holy temple, His kingdom, His community of life. He once again desires to lay bare His holy arm in the eyes of all nations, to build up His Body into that perfected temple of His name. Only such a temple will transparently declare His glory to the ends of the earth.

Now we're prepared to see a glorious prophecy that foretells of a day that is even now dawning upon us when Yahweh will once again reveal His holy temple and lay bare His right arm, but this time through Zion, His *corporate* Body, His church. This is what the words of Isaiah 52 point to:

"Awake, awake! Put on your strength, O Zion; put on your beautiful garments, O Jerusalem, the holy city! For the uncircumcised and the unclean shall no longer come to you. Shake yourself from the dust, arise; sit down, O Jerusalem! Loose yourself from the bonds of your neck, O captive daughter of Zion! Now therefore, what have I here," says the Lord, "that My people are taken away for nothing? Those who rule over them make them wail," says the Lord, "and My name is blasphemed continually every day. Therefore My people shall know My name; therefore they shall know in that day that I am He who speaks: 'Behold, it is I'" (Isa. 52:1-2, 5-6).

—Right Hand of Power

Vessels of Honor

When the potter takes the shapeless lump of clay, it, like the earth itself in the beginning, is "without form and void." It lacks all meaning and significance in terms of its relationship to us. Yet as the wheel spins, as hands bear down to press and shape the clay, as the clay takes on form, it suddenly assumes meaning and purpose. In other words, it *becomes* a cup, a vase, a bowl, a pitcher. A lump of inert matter has been *separated* from its natural surroundings and then shaped into a definitive form, which further distinguishes and separates it—even the wall of the pot is a wall of separation.

With believers, whatever form our lives assume as we spin under the press of providential hands serves to separate us for some purpose of God in the sacred pavilion. Like the material clay separated into a form, it now has meaning and purpose. And it is this separation coming from form that gives our lives significance. So the Spirit broods over the deep in our lives. It forms and shapes us into vessels of service for God's purpose, fashioning us into members of His Body "fitly framed together." Then He places the form of our covenant relationship, like a ceramic figurine, into the kiln of life's inevitable trials—including sorrows, pain, tragedies, persecutions, hardships. These will then fire and harden us in the enduring and durable forms into which His love has shaped our lives as vessels of honor for His *eternal* purpose.

—*Love That Works*

How can we remain faithful and see love "made complete among us" (1 John 4:17, NIV)? John tells us that love can be

---

Gen. 1:2

made complete in us—it can prove its enduring power as it did in Ruth's life—because "we *know* and *rely on* the love God has for us" (1 John 4:16, NIV). But John went on to also add that "love is made complete among us . . . *because in this world we are like Him*" (1 John 4:17, NIV). The natural inclination of fallen humanity resists any restraint of the covenant. So only through the outworking of God's Spirit-impelled Word in our hearts, making us increasingly "like Him," can we experience the oneness that covenant promises.

—*Committed to Love*

The Aquifer of Love

Someplace else, in some time past, or even right now somewhere high on a spiritual mountaintop, the waters of prayer and love and decent conduct and kind deeds and sacrificial service were, or now are, flowing. They've trickled down the mountain some distance and then slipped underground, as these streams so often do. Now, unseen, they're flowing down the mountain slope, then down the foothills, the plains and finally into the desert wasteland where you may now have found yourself. There's no visible sign of water as far as you can see. And you're parched. But the underground aquifers are nonetheless filling up.

All throughout history those who have been faithfully obedient to the love and kindness and goodness of God have been sending rivulets and trickles and drops into the great unseen reservoir of love. And the aquifers beneath the desert kingdoms of this world are filling. And you don't know what particle your own little obedience, your own small deed, your word, your prayer, your gift, might contribute to the filling of this underground reservoir—maybe you're doing nothing—but the reservoir is still filling. Yes, it's true that as you gaze across the sun-baked flatness, the place where you stand may still look just like a desert. But somewhere the desert rock is porous; and a deep thirst comes to you out in your desert, and it occurs just at a spot where the sand looks just slightly damp. And as you fall to your knees and begin frantically digging, the ground grows moister, then muddy; then it begins to bubble. And a thrill rises in your soul, for you know that the invisible aquifer has risen to touch the surface in just this spot where you are standing; and water will soon break forth from the desert in one of those unexpected miracles of life. And an angel of the Lord will come with an annunciation that the kingdom of God is at hand. And then it is up to you to decide whether you will drink from these waters or not.

It's not the *immediate* effectiveness of your deed or word or hope that you must look to. Oh, no—you must, in fact, let that be lost, all those little drops, into the great rivers and reservoirs of God's love. And then you must let that love in itself become its own reward as you unqualifiedly give yourself wholly to God, give yourself completely to do and obey His will in *everything*, believing that the reservoirs are filling up and that one day a stream in the desert will break forth at just the right time and in just the right place for just the right people and that you will be there—a part of that people.

—*Only Two Choices*

Dying to Distraction

Zeal for Your house has consumed me, and the reproaches of those who reproach You have fallen on me.

—Psalms 69:9

In an age of bewildering technological wizardry, we could say that people's souls are being destroyed by "weapons" of mass distraction. That is why you must truly die to these distractions before you can clearly hear, and then precisely know, just what the call and will of God is in your life. This death comes with a life-changing repentance and baptism into Christ's own death, a baptism that constitutes your pledge that the death you've died in regard to your fallen flesh will *keep* that flesh in the grave for the rest of your life as that life is lived in Christ on earth. That *is* your duty—to uphold your pledge: your pledge to die to selfishness, your pledge to love God and all your companions in God, your pledge to live for God and for your bona fide Christian companions, to live within and love the Christian social ethic, to conform to Christ's life by walking in the Holy Spirit.

If you do all this, you will not only uphold your pledge, but you'll also see *why* you *must* do so.

—Do You Really Mean It?

Words to Stand By

Without the reality of a covenant community, without the interweaving of lives, of commitments, of obligations—that is, without chesed—*genuine fulfillment in life remains forever elusive.*

—Love That Works

In sharing *chesed*, we must give ourselves to the Lord first, sacrificing ourselves to Him (Rom. 12:1-3) by sacralizing our lives into His own self-sacrificing love in His self-sacrificing people. This means we must then lay down our lives in a living and daily sacrament of love-service for our brothers, just as Jesus commanded. So we must speak words of commitment both to God and to our brothers according to the purposes and vision that God has given His Body and then stand by our word and keep the covenant.

We must be men and women of *chesed*—of mercy, loving-kindness, faithfulness, loyalty, integrity, truth, steadfast love, covenant keeping. Only God can give us the power to be such people. But He stands waiting to see who will speak words that carry us out into a faith that is motivated by love, keeping *chesed*, making our commitment, our obligation, standing by the words we've spoken.

When is the time to do this?—The time is when you hear His voice: "*Today, if you hear His voice*" (Heb. 3:7, 15). If you hear His Voice speaking to you today, then you must drop all and respond to His voice *now*—you must speak words to stand by *now* according to the Word He is speaking to you *now*. If you hear "a voice behind you, saying, 'This is the way; walk in it'" (Isa. 30:20-21, NIV), then by all and

---

2 Cor. 8:4-5; John 15:13; 1 John 3:16

every means respond, and do so immediately, before that Voice fades away in its intensity and once again becomes only "business as usual." For this is the Voice of the Bridegroom calling and showing you the way to His marriage altar, and He may call only once at your door before He moves on to those who will respond wholeheartedly to His love.

So if His love knocks at the door of your heart, don't "confer with flesh and blood," but "immediately" respond and speak words to stand by. The arm of heaven is extended to escort you to the altar of an eternal marriage covenant.

—Love That Works

Song of Sol. 5:2-6; Gal. 1:15-16

About the Author

Blair C. Adams was born January 5, 1944, in El Paso, Texas, at Hotel Dieu Hospital, a few blocks from the Rio Grande River and Old Mexico. Ever after, Blair remained fond of the desert, brightly sunlit places, desert peoples, great blue skies, austere mountains of serrated purple rock with little or no vegetation and a land of little rain. His distant ancestors came to America in the 1600's. More recent ancestors consisted of a long line of Texas frontiersmen, farmers and ranchers who first left their Tennessee farms just below the Cumberland Plateau and came to the Lone Star State in covered wagons in the 1850's. They pioneered and ranched all along the Red River from Lamar County on out to Hardeman County at the foot of the Panhandle Caprock, then over the Llano Estacado and eastern New Mexico to Las Cruces and El Paso.

Early Years

Some of Blair's fondest early memories were visits to the ranch of his older cousins, Elmer and Delia Connelley, near Las Cruces, New Mexico, where he first (hesitantly) sat a horse at the age of three. His early school years were spent in Amarillo and Lubbock, Texas. His first paying job was as a grocery store sack boy at the age of eleven. At thirteen, he switched to a newspaper delivery route, and at fourteen, he worked unloading and loading railroad boxcars and freight trucks at a large Lubbock warehouse. At sixteen, he worked for a while at an Indian trading post on the outskirts of Albuquerque, New Mexico, then as a soda "jerk" and short-order cook in a large combination drugstore, fountain and cafe. All the while, and over the next few years, he spent his off-school time doing ranch work, as a never-fully-accomplished cowboy. He also did construction work, including residential housing, public schools and buildings at Texas Tech University. This work mostly entailed manual labor digging ditches, putting up and taking down scaffolding on multi-storied buildings, carrying wheelbarrows of cement for bricklayers, cleanup and the like.

Education and Formative Life Events

Blair enrolled at Texas Tech in 1962 in the architectural and applied arts school. His grandmother had been a teacher and professional artist for many years, and since his childhood, he had passionately given himself to art, even winning a few awards, mostly in portraiture or ranch scenes and landscapes. Tech did not have a fine arts department at the time, so the next year Blair transferred to the University of Texas and moved to Austin. The following year, 1964, his father violently took his own life, and this dramatically redirected Blair's life. He found it difficult to concentrate on his studies, but kept trying to stumble along, distracted by the abiding grief of his father's tragic passing. He changed majors several times in hopes of finding answers to real-life questions that now troubled him more and more deeply. He finally ended up in the philosophy department. He had lost what little nominal or conceptual faith about God that he had.

In August of 1966, after three and a half years of college, Blair was drafted into the army during the heat of the Vietnam War. He was offered a position in Army intelligence in the American Security Associates, which worked directly under the National Security Agency. But he had to enlist for two more years because of the need for extended training and the obtaining of a "top secret crypto" security clearance, which was required for ASA personnel. He did so and was then stationed in Bavaria, West Germany, for three years, working in electronic intelligence to monitor activities of the Soviet Union and its Warsaw Pact satellites.

Upon being honorably discharged from military service, Blair reentered the philosophy department at the University of Texas for the summer and fall of 1970. But in January and February of 1971, Blair had a number of life-changing encounters with God. These convinced him that Jesus was God incarnate, that there was only one God and that this God held out the promise of a powerful spiritual experience to all believers. Blair also saw the possibility of a life lived in sustained relationship with God through Christ and in His Body, the church.

Ministry and Vision for Christian Community

Blair soon became a minister. He married Regina Mae McDanel on May 7, 1971. They then began ministering almost nightly in different churches around the country. They did this for the next two and a half years, when they would answer a call to move to New York City. But prior to

About the Author

that call, in the early years of his ministry, Blair began to lose any remaining notions he might have had of the church prospering by merely serving an adjunct and peripheral chaplaincy function for a larger American civil religion. He loved the country of his birth and of his ancestry, and he prayed for it and its leaders, but he did not believe he should worship a State. He did not believe nationalistic patriotism should become his religion, taking the place of God and His kingdom. He instead came to see the church as synonymous with life in an alternative to the world's smoldering cultures, an alternative called the "kingdom of God." This was, in Jesus' words, a "kingdom not of this world." Nonetheless, Blair saw in Scripture that this kingdom was to be "advancing" and that believers should pray that it would "come on earth as it is in heaven."

Blair did not, however, see this as any sort of political kingdom based on coercing others. Rather, it was the nonviolent and noncoercive rule of God's love, not only in individual lives but in an entire community of peoples from across the whole earth. These were people, however, held together only by their own commitment to this supernatural love and vision. They were "the people of God" in the sense that they had chosen to answer God's call to a distinct identity and purpose as God's people. They were to constitute a culture of life that served as an alternative to cultures maintained only by war and death. Whereas individuals, communities and whole nations were outsourcing to unknown others all that was essential to maintaining life—food, shelter, clothing, vocations, education and so on—and thereby becoming dependent on these unknown others, Blair envisioned local communities where everyone deeply knew one another and provided for the essentials of life themselves. Blair, eventually recognizing through his studies that many of these values were common to certain branches of the Anabaptist heritage of Christianity, nurtured the church in the Biblical convictions of nonviolence and simplicity of lifestyle that were part of that lineage. As a result, many from among the Anabaptist faith would come to affirm that the churches Blair has helped to build are vitally connected to the core beliefs of the Anabaptist tradition.

Blair continued to believe that the kingdom of God was to unfold "on earth as it is in heaven" (to quote from Jesus' model prayer), finding its embodiment in the sacralized life of Christian community. Such a community, like any living thing, would be whole. Thus Blair saw that it had to become an entire environment and culture, a vital way of seeing and being that affected all thinking, feelings, attitudes, labors, conduct and relationships of those who chose to freely participate in such an unfolding community. It would even affect people's relationship to land and work. No part of life would have to be lived outside of God and His purpose. In short, it would include all that is essential to life. Blair's abiding motive was always to participate in the creation of what has been called "communities of exemplary Christian existence."[48] He saw these communities as the crucial means to "teach us how to live authentically" in the presence of God and other people.[49] Blair hoped such communities would make wise choices possible in religion, culture, relationships, vocations and lifestyle, and "on a scale large enough to make a difference" in an increasingly troubled world.[50] In these communities, children, women and men would share the ineffable delight of experientially knowing God. And word and deed would be fused in the authentic unity of a lived life.

It is true that, from the beginning, Blair, Regina and their friends always saw the church not institutionally but as "the people of God." Moreover, from their very first days as Christians they talked of the church and kingdom in terms of a community of life. They also had even fully embraced nonviolence from their initial entrance into the kingdom. Nonetheless, it is also true that it would have been difficult to envision exactly how these things would unfold when, in the summer of 1973, Blair and Regina first moved into the Lower East Side slums of Manhattan. There they started a small mission church, Voice in the Wilderness. It was located on the same block that, at the time, the *New York Daily News* described as a virtual "pornorama of vice."[51] Yet from those early struggles and inauspicious beginnings has grown Heritage Ministries and the Homestead Heritage community of Waco, Texas. Homestead Heritage is now visited by over 250,000 people a year. All of its ministries and offshoot communities, traditional crafts, educational and other services now extend across the country and around the world. The combined communities enjoy over half a million visitors annually.

Writings

From early on in his ministry, Blair recognized that writing would be an integral part of his labors. He read and studied his entire adult life about the impact of ideas on individuals, human cultures and whole peoples. And it grieved him to see how these ideas often ended up controlling in pernicious ways the thinking, desires and actions of people who knew little or nothing about the ideas themselves. His desire therefore was to see these largely hidden cultural assumptions brought into the light, so that people could more freely make real, informed choices about the things that matter most in life. So, since a time of drought demands digging deeper wells to reach the sources, Blair wrote both extensively and intensively on these and related issues.

Finally, intentional communities like Homestead Heritage do not happen accidentally or as the result of wishful thinking. There are innumerable perils and pitfalls, any one of which can destroy a community. So Blair wrote probing books and monographs (over 250 titles) on how stable, enduring communities may be formed and sustained. His books are published by Colloquium Press in Elm Mott, Texas.

In February of 2015, Blair was diagnosed with an aggressive cancer, a form of non-Hodgkin lymphoma. Blair worked steadily to prepare the church and especially its leaders for his inevitable departure, all the while battling cancer and a failing heart. As his strength declined, he gave specific instructions for some yet unfinished writings and for the administration of the church he'd founded. Finally, he chose to spend most of his remaining time with his family. Six and a half years after his diagnosis, Blair's physical struggles were over, and he passed peacefully away in his own home surrounded by his devoted wife of fifty years and large family.

Blair's wife Regina, with whom he raised ten children, continues to live in Waco, Texas, surrounded by their children, grandchildren and many lifelong friends. Many of these relationships are now approaching the half a century mark.

Blair and Regina, 2015

Bibliography

Below are the titles of the books/series used to compile this devotional. All are written by Blair Adams and published by Colloquium Press. See our online bookstore at: homesteadheritage.com/books

All or Nothing?
Building Communities That Last

Aporia and the Collapse of Cultures
The Cultural Shift That Birthed Modernity, and the Shift That Is Coming

Building Christian Character
A Devotional Guidebook through the Elements of Christian Character for Children and Adults

The Church in the Time of Lawlessness

Coming into Orbit
Discovering Our Place within God's Living Order

Committed to Love

Conviction—Possessed by Saving Faith

Covenant Love
Inclusive or Exclusive?

Craft
The Art of Work

Culture, Agriculture and the Land

Do You Really Mean It?

Dying to Death: Repentance Series
Volume One: The Turning Point
Volume Two: Total Repentance
Volume Three: Taking the First Step: Acknowledgment
Volume Four: Acknowledging God's Word
Volume Five: Confession
Volume Six: Forsaking Sin
Volume Seven: Bedrock

Education Exodus
Leaving behind the Coercion of the Mind, Volume One

Everyday Miracles

An Exodus
A Journey toward a Culture of Life—Video

Experiencing God

Falling Is Not Flying
Why the Present Political-Economic Paradigm Is Not Aerodynamically Sound and Can Only Crash

False Faith versus Saving Faith

Forming Christ's Body: Book One
The Order for Perfecting Christ's Life and Love in His People
Restoring God's Living Order

A Garden Enclosed
A Culture Nurturing Covenant Love

Givens and Losses
On Losing Rehoboth

How Do You Know?

"Is Grandpa Saved?"
Reconciling Two Models of Salvation: Justification, Regeneration or Both?

The Island
A Parable of the Cuban Revolution

A Journey Home—Video

Koinonia Country
Sketches of Home and Community Life

Leaving the Lonely Labyrinth
Seeking Enduring Love as the Only Rule of Life in an Age of Narcissism and Manipulation, Betrayal and Cynicism, Violence and Ephemeral Connections

Life Against Death
The Struggle for Sustainable Communities: From Gandhi to Today

Love, Real Love

Love That Works
How the Ancient Hebrew Concept of Chesed *Creates Marriages, Families and Communities of Covenantal Love That Endure*

The Messianic Incarnation, Ancient Judaism and the Oneness of God
The Bedrock of the Only Sustainable Life—a Life "Sustained by the Word of His Power": An Abridgment

The Minister's Dialectical Handbook of Theology and Doctrine On the Holy Spirit
Substantive Answers for Serious Seekers

My Father's Child—Video

The Mystery of God

Nonviolence
A Challenge to Today's Christianity

Only Two Choices
Two Powers, Two Kingdoms, Two Worlds

The Preciousness of Death—A Baptismal Message about Salvation

The Right Hand of Power and the Name of Yahweh
How God Begins to Create a Community to Bear His Identity and Life on Earth

Salvation as Exodus
Seeing Redemption in More Than Individual Terms

Seeking the Eternal Universal

Servants of Love
Finding Our Place in the Body

So-o-o-o Emotional
Quantum Physics, Neuroscience and the Acquisition, Ordering and Channeling of Deep and Transcendent Emotion—A Primitive Christian Perspective

So You Want Community?

The Supernatural Power of Greed
How Christianity Has Been Co-opted

A Time of Harvest
Life on the Land in a Time of Birthings

Tolerance, Externalism and Holiness
Do Modesty and Gender-Specific Dress Represent the Simplicity of Holiness or Legalistic Intolerance? An Exploration into How to Escape Being Controlled by a Consumerist Culture

Truth as Song

Two Gospels—Video

Two Ways of Knowing
Theocentric versus Anthropocentric

What Makes Your Church So Different?
A Very Partial but Crucial Answer

What Kind of Family?
Innovative Myths, Traditional Religion and the Art of Human Relationships: A Partisan Survey of Contrasting Configurations and the Possibility of Healing Today's Families

What's the Problem with Love?
Love's Counterfeits, Its Nature and Its Source

What We Believe
A Synopsis of the Vision, Spiritual Roots and Cultural Position of Heritage Ministries

Why Build Agrarian Christian Communities?

Why We Live in Community
Intentional Community and the Survival of the Church

Wisdom's Children: Book One
Home Education and the Creation of Communities That Sustain Life
Necessity and Possibility

Wisdom's Children: Book Two
A Philosophy of Christian Knowledge and Learning for the Education of Complete Individuals and for the Forming of an Integral Christian Community Life
General Principles

Copyright Notices

Scripture quotations marked NKJV are from the New King James Version. Copyright© 1982 by Thomas Nelson, Inc. Used by permission. All rights reserved.

Scripture quotations marked NASB are from the New American Standard Bible. Copyright © 1960, 1962, 1963, 1968, 1971, 1972, 1973, 1975, 1977, 1995 by The Lockman Foundation. Used by permission.

Scripture quotations marked NIV are taken from the Holy Bible, New International Version®. Copyright © 1973, 1978, 1984, 2011 by Biblica, Inc.™ Used by permission of Zondervan. All rights reserved worldwide.

Scripture quotations marked Ampl. are from the Amplified Bible. Copyright © 1954, 1958, 1962, 1964, 1965, 1987 by The Lockman Foundation. Used by permission.

Scripture quotations marked KJV are from the King James Version, public domain.

Endnotes

1. Johannes P. Louw et al., eds., *Greek-English Lexicon of the New Testament: Based on Semantic Domains*, 2nd ed. (New York: United Bible Societies, 1989), p. 6.

2. H. Richard Niebuhr, *Christ and Culture* (New York: Harper and Row Publishers, Harper Torchbooks, 1975), p. 32.

3. Don E. Saliers, *The Soul in Paraphrase: Prayer and the Religious Affections* (New York: Seabury Press, A Crossroad Book, 1980), p. 12.

4. Michael Harper, *Equal and Different: Male and Female in Church and Family* (London: Hodder and Stoughton, 1994), p. 21.

5. Harper, *Equal and Different*, p. 21.

6. Søren Kierkegaard, *Kierkegaard's Concluding Unscientific Postscript*, trans. David F. Swenson, ed. Walter Lowrie (Princeton, N.J.: Princeton University Press, 1941), p. 182.

7. Everett Ferguson, *Backgrounds of Early Christianity* (Grand Rapids, Mich.: William B. Eerdmans Publishing Co., 1987), pp. 331-33; William Barclay, trans., *The Gospel of John*, vol. 2 (Philadelphia: Westminster Press, 1956), pp. 278-80; Will Durant, *Caesar and Christ: A History of Roman Civilization and of Christianity from Their Beginnings to A.D. 325*, part 3 of *The Story of Civilization* (New York: Simon and Schuster, 1944), p. 571.

8. Frederick Mayer, *Education for a New Society* (Bloomington, Ind.: Phi Delta Kappa Educational Foundation, 1973), p. 16.

9. Mayer, *Education for a New Society*, p. 16.

10. Dorothy L. Sayers, "The Lost Tools of Learning," *Journal of Christian Reconstruction*, Summer 1977, p. 25.

11. Merrill F. Unger, *Unger's Bible Dictionary* (Chicago: Moody Press, 1966), p. 1177.

12. *Encyclopaedia Britannica Macropaedia*, 15th ed., s.v., "Christianity"; A. James Gregor, *The Ideology of Fascism: The Rationale of Totalitarianism* (New York: Free Press, 1969), p. 333; John Passmore, *The Perfectibility of Man* (New York: Charles Scribner's Sons, 1970), p. 213.

13. Sara E. Melzer, *Discourses of the Fall: A Study of Pascal's "Pensées"* (Berkeley, Calif.: University of California Press, 1986), p. 1 (emphasis added).

14. *Encyclopaedia Britannica Online* (2009), s.v. "quantum mechanics," https://www.britannica.com/science/quantum-mechanics-physics (emphasis added).

15. Michael Polanyi and Harry Prosch, *Meaning* (Chicago: University of Chicago Press, 1975), pp. 36-37.

16. Jeffrey Satinover, *Cracking the Bible Code* (New York: William Morrow and Co., 1997), p. 239 (emphasis in original).

17. Satinover, *Cracking the Bible Code*, p. 239 (emphasis added).

18. Satinover, *Cracking the Bible Code*, pp. 239-40.

19. John Archibald Wheeler, "Bohr, Einstein, and the Strange Lesson of the Quantum," in *Mind in Nature*, ed. Richard Q. Elvee (San Francisco: Harper and Row Publishers, 1982), pp. 13, 16-21.

20. Satinover, *Cracking the Bible Code*, p. 240 (emphasis in original).

21. Satinover, *Cracking the Bible Code*, p. 243.

22. D. M. Dooling, "The Alchemy of Craft," in *A Way of Working*, ed. D. M. Dooling (New York: Parabola Books, 1986), p. 99.

23. Marcel Proust, *The Past Recaptured*, trans. Frederick A. Blossom (New York: Albert and Charles Boni, 1932), p. 237.

24. Mike Mason, *The Mystery of Marriage: Meditations on the Miracle* (Sisters, Oreg.: Multnomah, 1985), pp. 167-68.

25. Mason, *The Mystery of Marriage*, p. 168.

26. Rudolf Otto, *The Idea of the Holy: An Inquiry into the Non-Rational Factor in the Idea of the Divine and Its Relation to the Rational*, trans. John W. Harvey (1923; reprint, London: Oxford University Press, 1958), pp. 12, 14-15, 26-29.

27. Otto, *The Idea of the Holy*, pp. 6-7.

28. Otto, *The Idea of the Holy*, pp. 26-27.

29. George Lakoff, *Don't Think of an Elephant! Know Your Values and Frame the Debate* (White River Junction, Vt.: Chelsea Green Publishing, 2004), p. xv (emphasis added).

30. Lakoff, *Don't Think of an Elephant!* p. xv (emphasis in original).

31. Lakoff, *Don't Think of an Elephant!* p. xv (emphasis added).

32. Heinrich Seesemann, in *Theological Dictionary of the New Testament*, ed. Gerhard Friedrich, trans. and ed. Geoffrey W. Bromiley, vol. 6 (Grand Rapids, Mich.: Wm. B. Eerdmans Publishing Co., 1968), pp. 484-85.

33. Seesemann, in *Theological Dictionary of the New Testament*, p. 485.

34. H. Norman Strickman and Arthur M. Silver, trans., *Ibn Ezra's Commentary on the Pentateuch: Exodus (Shemot)* (New York: Menorah Publishing Co., 1996), p. 561; Judah Goldin, trans., *The Fathers according to Rabbi Nathan* (New York: Schocken Books, 1974), pp. 127-28.

35. Nathaniel Lande, M*indstyles, Lifestyles: A Comprehensive Overview of Today's Life-Changing Philosophies* (Los Angeles: Price/Stern/Sloan, 1976), p. 457.

36. William Shakespeare, "The Tragedy of Hamlet, Prince of Denmark," in *The Complete Works of William Shakespeare*, ed. John Dover Wilson (London: Octopus Books, 1980), p. 896.

37. Nathaniel Lande, "Interview: R. Buckminster Fuller," in *Mindstyles/ Lifestyles: A Comprehensive Overview of Today's Life-Changing Philosophies* (Los Angeles: Price/Stern/Sloan Publishers, 1976), p. 457.

38. Michael Allen Gillespie, *The Theological Origins of Modernity* (Chicago: University of Chicago Press, 2008), pp. 12-13; C. Hugh Holman and William Harmon, *A Handbook to Literature*, 5th ed. (New York: Macmillan Publishing Co., 1986), p. 34.

39. Gillespie, *The Theological Origins of Modernity*, p. 13.

40. Václav Havel, "The Need for Transcendence in the Postmodern World," *Futurist*, July-August 1995, p. 46.

41. Havel, "Need for Transcendence in the Postmodern World," p. 46.

42. Havel, "Need for Transcendence in the Postmodern World," pp. 46-49; Gillespie, *The Theological Origins of Modernity*, p. 13.

43. Havel, "Need for Transcendence in the Postmodern World," p. 47.

44. M. Francis Mannion, "Modern Culture and the Monastic Paradigm," *Communio: International Catholic Review*, Fall 1993, p. 504.

45. Mannion, "Modern Culture and the Monastic Paradigm," p. 504.

46. Bill McKibben, *The Age of Missing Information* (New York: A Plume Book, 1993), p. 185.

47. Wendell Berry, *Standing by Words* (San Francisco: North Point Press, 1983), p. 205.

48. Mannion, "Modern Culture and the Monastic Paradigm,", p. 504.

49. Mannion, "Modern Culture and the Monastic Paradigm," p. 504.

50. McKibben, *The Age of Missing Information*, p. 185.

51. Lawrie Mifflin, "Call E. 14th St. a Pornorama of Vice," *Daily News* (New York), 9 July 1975.

Acknowledgments

We would like to thank the following people whose assistance made the production of this book possible:

Production coordinators: Dan Lancaster and Camille Allensworth

Editing and Organizing: Isaac French coordinator; Evan Birdsong, Simeon Cunningham, Helen French, Dan Lancaster and Matthew Pressly

Typesetting: Gail Gardner, coordinator; Cary Jennings

Checking: Camille Allensworth and Lisa Bradford, coordinators

Proofreading: Marcia Bench, coordinator; Grace Brydon

Research and references: Deanne Ballerino and Marian Smith, coordinators; Omie Muir

Scripture references: Nathan Tittley, coordinator

Cover design: Asahel Adams

Technical Support: Ben Owen

Made in the USA
Monee, IL
05 December 2024

1423a6b6-efbe-4491-8b8d-29f93579e14bR01